MARY

✻

Kathy Coffey

Maryknoll, New York 10545

Founded in 1970, Orbis Books endeavors to publish works that enlighten the mind, nourish the spirit, and challenge the conscience. The publishing arm of the Maryknoll Fathers and Brothers, Orbis seeks to explore the global dimensions of the Christian faith and mission, to invite dialogue with diverse cultures and religious traditions, and to serve the cause of reconciliation and peace. The books published reflect the views of their authors and do not represent the official position of the Maryknoll Society. To learn more about Maryknoll and Orbis Books, please visit our website at www.maryknollsociety.org.

Queries regarding rights and permissions should be addressed to:
Orbis Books, P.O. Box 308, Maryknoll, NY 10545-0308.

Manufactured in the United States of America.

Library of Congress Cataloging-in-Publication Data

Coffey, Kathy.
    Mary / Kathy Coffey.
       p. cm. – (Catholic spirituality for adults)
    Includes bibliographical references.
    ISBN 978-1-57075-724-2 (pbk.)
    1. Mary, Blessed Virgin, Saint. 2. Catholic Church – Doctrines.
  I. Title.
    BT603.C64 2009
    232.91 – dc22

                                    2008034416

MARY

Catholic Spirituality for Adults

General Editor
Michael Leach

Other Books in the Series

Prayer by Joyce Rupp
Reconciliation by Robert Morneau
Holiness by William J. O'Malley
Diversity of Vocations by Marie Dennis
Eucharist by Robert Barron
Charity by Virgil Elizondo

For the Nazareth group,
dear companions on the journey.

*"Life is short and we have not too much time
for gladdening the hearts of those who are
traveling the dark way with us."*
— Henri Amiel

And for the staff
at Sacred Heart Jesuit Retreat House,
Sedalia, Colorado,
where some of this book was written.

"Windows look out on mountains and the walls are kind."
— May Sarton

Contents

Contents

Introduction to Catholic Spirituality for Adults

C ATHOLIC SPIRITUALITY FOR ADULTS explores the deepest dimension of spirituality, that place in the soul where faith meets understanding. When we reach that place we begin to see as if for the first time. We are like the blind man in the Gospel who could not believe his eyes: "And now I see!"

Catholicism is about seeing the good of God that is in front of our eyes, within us, and all around us. It is about learning to see Christ Jesus with the eyes of Christ Jesus, the Way, the Truth, and the Life.

Only when we *see* who we are as brothers and sisters of Christ and children of God can we begin to *be* like Jesus and walk in his Way. "As you think in your heart, so you are" (Prov. 23:7).

Catholic Spirituality for Adults is for those of us who want to make real, here and now, the words we once learned in school. It is designed to help us go beyond information to transformation. "When I was a child, I spoke as a child, I understood as a child, I thought as a child, but when I became an adult, I put away childish things" (1 Cor. 13:11).

The contributors to the series are the best Catholic authors writing today. We have asked them to explore the deepest dimension of their own faith and to share with us what they are learning to see. Topics covered range from prayer — "Be

still, and know that I am God" (Ps. 46:10) — to our purpose
in life — coming to know "that God has given us eternal life,
and this life is in his Son" (1 John 5:11) — to simply getting
through the day — "Put on compassion, kindness, humility,
gentleness, and patience" (Col. 3:12).

Each book in this series reflects Christ's active and loving
presence in the world. The authors celebrate our membership
in the mystical body of Christ, help us to understand our
spiritual unity with the entire family of God, and encourage us
to express Christ's mission of love, peace, and reconciliation
in our daily lives.

Catholic Spirituality for Adults is the fruit of a publishing partnership between Orbis Books, the publishing arm of
the Catholic Foreign Mission Society of America (Maryknoll),
and RCL Benziger, a leading provider of religious and family life education for all ages. This series is rooted in vital
Catholic traditions and committed to a continuing standard
of excellence.

Michael Leach
General Editor

Author's Introduction:
A Dialogue with Mary

Kathy: Mary, you're a muddle. I guess it sounds better to say a "mystery," but that word dignifies my bewilderment. There's a lot I don't understand about you. You've inspired the noblest poetry and the worst sentimentality, lovely hymns and banal doggerel, transcendent sculpture and embarrassingly bad art. Where in the accumulation over centuries of devotion is the true identity of a girl who changed the world with her "yes"? What should I say about you in this book?

Mary: Start with what we have in common, because that's something you know. Write what you've lived: being a woman and mother, loving your child more than life, getting frustrated with that same beloved child, seeking balance, peace, and beauty, aging, watching your child mature, experiencing the human mix of joy and pain.

Make me relevant to people like yourself: stressed, hassled, worried, but still wanting to give their one, cherished life their best shot. As you already know, most authors are talking to themselves in their books. So say what you as author need to hear.

K: I guess if I'd ever had a big sister, that would come close to describing you. Someone who had gracefully negotiated the befuddling world of growing up, transitioning into adolescence, then adulthood, making the most of the time she had. Someone serene, as I picture you, compassionate, and wonderfully funny. I could walk into her kitchen any time and she'd have the coffee ready. I could tell her anything.

M: And she wouldn't dump advice on you. It would be the best kind of conversation, which didn't make you feel stupid. Except, now and then, a succinct little chop would remind you to aim higher, be better.

K: How do I make you a genuine presence people would invite to walk through their days beside them?

M: A lot of folks already have Presences. They try to figure out a new situation by What Mom Would Do Here, or where is my better angel leading me? If I could talk to my best friend right now, what would she say?

Sometimes when you're stressed, summoning that presence is the first step toward peace. The word "alone" terrifies humans because they don't know how false it really is.

I'm the answer to that loneliness, which is way better than being someone in a history book or even a sacred text. I'm alive and present *right now,* whatever swamp — or sanctuary — you're in. Yes, God is there too, so think of me as God's feminine, sisterly face.

K: It is wonderfully supportive to have a hidden, constant companion. But I get easily overwhelmed by the enormity of this task: sifting through volumes of literature, trying to distill it into one short book. You've inspired enough literature to fill many libraries and enough art to fill several museums. Do you ever trip over all your titles?

M: Don't let that get in your way. Use as your selection principle whatever would help someone like yourself. You're weighing a long and universal tradition against the immediate, personal need. But I will be for you and your readers what I have always been for Christians: a model of trust, of humans at their best. My voice reminds you that you're splendid. I summon your best self, saying, "This is who you most deeply are: beloved. That's all that matters. Now act like it."

K: I could listen to that voice forever, because there's no trace of whine in it, or numbing repetition. When I goof up, it reminds me I'm just not myself. When I achieve, it points to the reason why. Your reminder is fresh as first morning, clean and beautiful as lake, snug as storytelling, stimulating as friends' conversation.

M: At the same time it is deeply familiar, like a voice you recognize on the phone from the first syllable. *Everybody* wants that: the advocate, gardener, model, cheerleader.

Helpers, rescuers, saviors, and moms sometimes lose track of who they really are. I'm the mirror that shows you your finest self.

K: "Mary as Mirror" rates a whole chapter, later on.... Somewhere along the line, we sophisticated sorts may have turned away from you because we cringed at the schmaltz, the soupy piety that sometimes clouds Marian devotion. I would never criticize another person's faith; I just couldn't claim it for myself. But now I wonder. In our "enlightenment," do we cheat ourselves of someone wonderful?

I've recently discovered Thérèse of Lisieux and something similar happened to her. A lot of that goo was layered onto her later and has little to do with the real person, who is gutsy, alive, bold, and definitely worth knowing.

M: It's the *not* knowing that's the impoverishment. Did it ever occur to you there's a reason you were given this topic, despite your being pitifully unqualified? Haven't you noticed how I always appear to simple, uneducated people, often children, in out-of-the-way places, never to world leaders or great scholars in impressive palaces or libraries of major cities? Grace slips through strange openings.

That's the miracle and mystery of me: how I adapt to everyone's needs at each particular time. Those folks who were so starved for the feminine in the Middle Ages found what they needed in me.

Now in the twenty-first century, as you try to carve out different roles for women, exploring your own place, surviving the daily grind, leaving some legacy, you'll turn to me and find what *you* need, as people always have.

K: That's the meaning of the maternal archetype, I suppose. Not that you're a chameleon changing colors, but the divine always intersects us where we are, with exactly what we need.

Funny, I didn't grow up with Marian devotion, never said the rosary, was usually surprised when a Marian feast rolled around, knew the art only slightly, and here I am, with all that unlikely background, writing a book about you.

M: Your skepticism serves me. There are lots of people like you. And a lot who want a marvelous Big Sister. I come to all ages in cahoots with Jesus. At a personal level, it's the caring, concerned phone call or the meal at your door when you need it.

On a larger stage, it's the breakthrough in medical research, the humane legislation, the court victory for justice, the literacy tutoring, the peace negotiations, the programs to end poverty and homelessness — I've got a finger in every one of those pies. "And my delight was to be with the children of human beings." Wherever they are hurting, I'm intervening. Wherever they succeed, I cheer.

Haven't you noticed how I always appear to simple, uneducated people, often children, in out-of-the-way places, never to world leaders or great scholars in impressive palaces or libraries of major cities?

K: The marvelous massage therapist I had yesterday, who knew exactly how to help and did it as ministry: soothing the pain, easing the tension, breathing *with* me, heating the towels, lightly touching muscles clenched tight as fist, teasing them to relax, telling me to quit *trying* because the trying was just another stress: she is a figure of Mary.

M: Oh, I'm everywhere: in grandmas and grandpas, nurses and therapists, prison guards and prisoners, artists and musicians, little kids and teenagers, wherever the Spirit of God flourishes and kindness happens. I get around.

K: I'm starting to see. Mary is for everyone who always wanted a best friend or strong "significant other" with a wise tenderness and a voice like cascading water, with the perfect blend of affirming sweetness and nudging challenge. We lean toward you because you're earthily human, close to our concerns, but at the same time, more: arcing beyond our limits, embracing earth *and* heaven, becoming our personal window to the divine. You show us what we could be.

M: Yes, dear. Slowly, you're catching on. I suppose you'll do....

K: Then let's get started.

Questions for Reflection or Discussion

- Who is Mary for you now?
- If you were to write a dialogue with her like the one above, what would you say?
- What do you think Mary would say?

Chapter One

Mary for All Seasons

M ARY IS A GUIDE THROUGH life's passages, because she moved through them herself. She knew firsthand how every season of life combines sadness and joy. Both themes interweave in her life as they do in ours.

Summer — The Beginning

The Early Sweetness

> ...*and the child grew in wisdom and age and grace.*
>
> (Luke 2:52)

In the seasonal metaphor, Mary's early motherhood corresponds to summer. Then the torrent of bird song, festival of flowers, abundance of color and fragrance speak eloquently of the life force, the lavish creativity of God. All is potential then; so much lies ahead. The main characters in the Gospel story are sweetly innocent, unaware of the chapters that follow.

The gentle appeal of Madonna and child touches something at our very core. She is young, and almost always portrayed as beautiful. The baby curled beside her is a fresh, dear presence as she cooks or carries water.

As Jesus grew older, Mary taught him the psalms and stories of their tradition. She passed along the customs of their culture with the same joy any mother hands on the best parts of her heritage.

Mary probably didn't guess how Jesus would transcend that Jewish birthright. He would lift it to new heights and transform his roots into a worldwide religion that would far surpass their small Mideastern sect.

But children must first be grounded. Mary gave Jesus his starting point, his launching pad. Summer is the time for planting, delighting in the first green shoots, the lacy leaves and petals. As Mary watched Jesus grow and mature, she must have been so proud, thrilled with his growing skills and insights.

The presence of an infant in a group of people attracts all the attention. Conversations hush and normally articulate people coo baby talk. They suspend thoughts of the future as all focus on the present, the gift of this child.

And yet for Jesus, as for all children, the summery season is too short.

Simeon's Warning

"Your own soul a sword shall pierce." (Luke 2:35)

Summer's warmth is shaded by its brevity, precariousness, the inevitably of shorter days, cooling temperatures and killing frost. So for Mary, over each happy, youthful day hung the shadow of Simeon's prediction after the presentation of the infant Jesus in the temple.

That day had begun with such bright promise, the pride of the new parents in their child, a rightness in observing the customary rituals. So Simeon's warning must have sliced their joy with a cutting edge. As one scholar writes:

> He has voiced something all the more terrible because it is voiced about love, that elusive treasure we all long for. Simeon shows us that all love is experienced in the shadow of the sword. Perhaps even more terrible is the fact that renouncing love does not free us from the sword. For if the price of loving somebody is the certainty of the eventual loss of that person, the price of refusing to love is the loss of our capacity to love and be loved. Thus, attempting to escape a sword, we are pierced by an even more terrible one.[1]

Lost or Found?

"Your father and I have been searching for you in great anxiety." (Luke 2:48)

That wrenching separation first foretold during Jesus' presentation in the temple became vivid reality when Jesus at the age of twelve was separated from his parents and remained in the temple (Luke 2:41–51). Was he lost there, or found? It's not unusual for preadolescents to give their parents coronaries. Yet something is unique about Jesus: his stay in the temple is different from other boys' death-defying pranks. He speaks with a confidence beyond most twelve-year olds, an unnerving brilliance that must have startled Mary, leaving her wondering what else lay ahead. That day when he conversed with the teachers must have hinted that he wouldn't simply take over Joseph's carpentry business. She would discover his hidden potential more fully in the next season.

Fall — The Harvest

Into a Larger World

Then he began to say to them, "Today this scripture has been fulfilled in your hearing." All spoke well of him and were amazed at the gracious words that came from his mouth. They said, "Is not this Joseph's son?"

(Luke 4:21–22)

Even knowing the patriarchal tone of temple society, it still seems odd that no one in the temple that day asked, "Is not this *Mary's* son?" All the seeds his mother had planted in Jesus' childhood came to full ripening in his public life. When he unrolled the scroll and proclaimed the text from Isaiah, then said, "This scripture has been fulfilled in your hearing," Mary may have felt a twinge of the crowd's bewilderment and consternation.

But she had another memory they did not have, of the first time she had told her young son the ancient hope of their people: that the lame might walk and the poor hear good news. Because the roots of Jewish faith are nurtured in the home, she would have been the one who introduced Jesus to Isaiah.

That day as he spoke in the synagogue, Mary remembered the first time he'd heard Isaiah in their home: his quickening interest, the light in his eyes as the passage kindled his calling. Perhaps Isaiah had resonated for him more clearly than any other book of Scripture. This connection had matured over the years, as he grew into an understanding of his mission. Knowing him so well, Mary probably also noticed a growing confidence, the same radical trust that mirrored her "fiat."

She alone knew he didn't need to *read* the scroll. Its words were written on his heart. What happened that day in the temple with the Isaiah passage would recur. The Magnificat, once sung as his lullaby, eventually took on another form as the Beatitudes. Jesus probably learned from Mary to respect women as few other men of his time and culture did. Examples abound of his love for Mary spilling into relationships with other women:

* His grave courtesy and compassion for the woman caught in adultery.

* His honesty with the Samaritan woman.

* His close friendship with Martha and Mary.

Indeed, those who knew him best recognized the traits he inherited from his mother.

Repudiation?

Then his mother and his brothers came; and standing outside, they sent to him and called him.... And he replied, "Who are my mother and my brothers?" Looking at those who sat around him, he said, "Here are my mother and my brothers! Whoever does the will of God is my brother and sister and mother." (Mark 3:31–35)

There's a sadness in autumn, the farewell to summer, the anticipation of winter ahead. In any human relationship, no matter how loving, estrangements and differences can occur. Mary and Jesus were fully human, so no strangers to that tension. He is taken from her and given to others, an ache balanced by realizing that was why he had been born. She had been blessed to have him so long and cherished the memories of those early years.

But she was human and she was sensitive. It's possible she felt that strangers had taken him from her. Mary was especially vulnerable after Joseph's death. In her culture, a widow's identity and livelihood depended on her son. She must have wondered where his road would end, and feared for his safety. She must have felt a sharp tension: it wouldn't be fair to keep him for herself alone, any more than we would hoard the abundant produce of the autumn garden. She must have been pulled in two directions: delighted that he'd found his mission to the larger world, saddened by the unknowns of where his path might lead.

Like any mother, Mary couldn't intervene. Jesus couldn't be deterred from confronting unjust authority. Once again, she was powerless. His preference for the poor, the audacity of his teaching, his questioning of the law's primacy were bound to land him in serious trouble. She knew that better than anyone.

During this season, Mary experiences the pang of letting go felt by all parents. It's summed up on a plaque found in the homes of young adults: "and just when they're fit to live with, they live with someone else." Scholars add another dimension: "Hurt goes deepest where love is its entry point."[2]

During the difficult seasons, we can empathize most with Mary's humanity. A young woman who starred in the play *Diary of Anne Frank* commented, "We had to show the characters' flaws. Their petulance, greed, and raw nerves were exacerbated when they had to live together in close quarters for a long time. If we didn't, they would become icons, too distant from real humans to matter." So too for Mary. Her anguish brings her closer to the struggles of ordinary human beings.

Most children leave home as a natural process. But painful separations occur when they break radically from their parents' values. At the worst extreme are teens who get involved with illegal drugs, alcohol, gangs, or criminal activity.

His preference for the poor, the audacity of his teaching, his questioning of the law's primacy were bound to land him in serious trouble. She knew that better than anyone.

For many years *A Woman Wrapped in Silence* was classic Marian poetry. Its author, John Lynch, describes this separation poetically, perhaps the only way it can be adequately addressed:

> She'd heard Him. She had heard
> These sentences and knew them. They were hers.
> She'd known they were to be and that they'd fall
> For her and were to be her own against
> A world of men that might be free in them,
> But could not own them, nor the pain in them
> As she would own....
>
> She was a woman here,
> A woman who had seen a long love close
> To her; who heard a sound that was an end
> Awaited, and who knew that no appeal

Or cry or staggering of hers could stay
This certainty, or turn again the sound
Until it still was only time expected
And not time begun. . . .

She was a woman
Who was made bereft, who felt a pall
Close suddenly upon a warmth that had
Been hers against a hundred lesser pains,
And now was gone.[3]

Winter — The Killing Frost

Their *Crucifixion*

*Now there stood by the cross of Jesus his mother, and
his mother's sister, Mary the wife of Cleophas, and Mary
Magdalene.* (John 19:25)

Mary enters into a wintry season as, finally, it lands: the sword
that Simeon predicted when her son was small. The threat
had hovered over her life for so long, they were not strangers
when it arrived. For a long time, she didn't know what shape
the evil would take, but she dreaded it. She had probably
seen thousands of crosses outside Jerusalem. They were the
tool of the Romans, a lingering threat to a subject people, the
constant warning: resist us and this is what you get.

But there's always a slight distance between what happens to other people and what affects us directly. Now,
horribly, Mary would bridge that gap. She saw the full bru-
tality: the long insult of Jesus' trial, the excruciating crown
of thorns and scourging, the arduous climb, dragging the
cross up Calvary. Then the sad end: her son, dearer than life,

crucified as a common criminal, hung between thieves, despised and scorned by both Roman oppressors and his own people. The sword that had hovered over her so long finally pierces his side: "and immediately there poured out blood and water."

John is less interested in the historical dimension of the crucifixion than in its symbolic implications. While Mary and the beloved disciple were historical figures, they are given an importance at Calvary that transcends two limited human beings.[4] By entrusting her to the beloved disciple, and him to her, Jesus makes Mary the mother of all those who would follow.

Mary participates in Jesus' suffering there just as she felt birth pains at Bethlehem. Thus Mary takes the role of "spiritual mother" to us all. For most of us, a pain-wracked death would prompt depression or anger at injustice. Jesus and Mary don't focus on their personal agony, but on loving and caring for future Christians. Thus their love assumes an "unparalleled power."[5]

The Wintry Season Today

The question of aging gracefully is a predicament now confronting many baby boomers, but it has been and will be an issue for every generation. As we watch those we once looked up to gradually growing bent and frail, losing their vibrancy and strength, we mourn for them as well as ourselves. "Margaret, are you grieving...?" Gerard Manley Hopkins asks a young girl in his poem "Spring and Fall." He finally concludes it's not the falling leaves that sadden her; rather: "It is the blight man was born for, / It is Margaret you mourn for."

As people age, death becomes a constant companion and funerals a regular event. Friends and relatives leave the immediacy of this life and enter the next. As the elderly recognize the proximity of their life's end, the finest people hone their focus to what's most important. With astonishing humility, they allow younger people to see their diminishment and shift graciously from care-givers to the ones cared for. We cannot gloss over the pain of this stage any more than we could minimize Mary's pain at Calvary. The losses and grief are real and excruciating.

But with God's grace, those who age well, learning to sacrifice graciously, achieve a wisdom that characterizes the last stage. No longer preoccupied with success or appearance, they can focus on what really matters: eternal truths, the purpose for which they were created, their passage into another life, and their most genuine identity.

Grandparents often shock their offspring by tolerating behavior in their grandchildren that they never would have permitted in their children. They become more relaxed about the rules, more intent on the individual. Perhaps that's because they've mastered the art of unrestricted love, seeing right past the annoying behavior to the beloved child. It's the *parents'* job to discipline; grandparents chuckle that they have the luxury of spoiling. After a certain age, people don't seem to worry much about polite niceties. They speak the truth, unsterilized.

When the dead Jesus rests at last in Mary's arms, a certain peace pervades. Every artist who has depicted this scene, especially Michelangelo in his *Pietà*, has shown beneath the torn limbs and the agony, a tortured beauty. Even in winter, some hope of spring stirs beneath the ice.

Spring — A New Birth

Jesus Reborn

"He is not here, but has risen." (Luke 24:5)

After a long winter of loss and cold, spring often surprises. A film of green suddenly tints the bleached, colorless landscape. Tulips, daffodils, crocus, and hyacinths shout with glad, outrageous colors. Hearts lighten; it's the time for street fairs, first communions, weddings, and graduations. "We've survived that lousy winter!" is the season's underlying theme.

The profusion of what Gerard Manley Hopkins in his poem "Spring" calls "all this juice and all this joy" is a dim shadow of what Jesus' resurrection must have meant to Mary. The thrill of seeing in color after seeing only in black and white doesn't begin to capture her first vision of him after his brutal death.

It represents an end to terrible, unnecessary deaths and sorrowing mothers. In the world according to God's plan, the resurrection stops all suffering. Mary had suffered long and unimaginably hard trials. For her, the springtime must have come in the new life of Jesus' followers. She must have delighted in their growth and maturation as she once did in his.

Pentecost

All these with one accord devoted themselves to prayer, together with the women and Mary the mother of Jesus.
(Acts 1:14–15)

Luke has not mentioned Mary at the cross, but he deliberately starts Acts with a reference to her presence with the disciples when the Holy Spirit comes. In a similar way, the Holy Spirit had overshadowed Mary at the Annunciation. Just as Christ was born in the Gospel, so the community has a new birth in Acts. Again, Mary plays a central role, this time helping to birth the church of Jerusalem.

Mary is a key transition figure for the early church, a witness to Jesus' infancy who continues into Acts. But she is not the only female member of the community who is active in spreading the good news. As Sister Elizabeth Johnson points out, overemphasizing Mary's role can cause us to overlook the importance of other women. Each had a distinctive relationship to Jesus and a unique ministry. All were on fire with a special energy because they had been ignited by the Spirit.[6]

There were certainly controversies in the early church (we hear a lot about the circumcision question). But even with those, that era must have had a spring-like quality, a sense of unlimited potential, the adventure of bringing long-awaited good news to a waiting, hungry world.

Questions for Reflection or Discussion

+ Which of the seasons in Mary's life do you identify with most strongly?

+ What season or seasons of life do you find yourself in now? (You can be in more than one at the same time.)

+ How could Mary guide you through this season, based on her experience of it?

+ What would you like to tell or ask her about it?

Chapter Two

A Cluster of Images

"THERE ARE NEVER ENOUGH names and images for what we love," wrote Dorothy Soelle.[7] Her words explain the enormous flowering of art, music, literature, and tradition about Mary. The Latin saying *De Maria numquam satis,* "about Mary there is never enough" explains this vast devotion. With such a richness of different interpretations and approaches, no one can claim to have complete or total truth. The winnowing or filtering process then becomes a matter of individual preference.

A historical survey is never enough; it must be complemented by "who Mary is for us." So in this cluster of images, I hope to find the facets of Mary most helpful to someone like me, a twenty-first-century mom who often gets preoccupied with the wrong stuff, but wants an inspiring model, a woman who understands my life from her own lived experience, firsthand.

Apprentice to God

And we to her. Mary is co-author with God of her story — as we all co-author our stories. When a woman from the crowd, obviously impressed with Jesus, calls out, "Blessed are the breasts that nursed you and the womb that bore you," he deflects the compliment. His response implies that there was far more to Mary's maternity than the physical. "Rather, blessed are they who hear the word of God and keep it" (Luke 11:27–28) shows that he knew two dimensions of Mary's inner life.

First, Mary heard. We already know from the comment in Luke 2:19 about her "treasuring all these things, pondering them in her heart," that she was a reflective person. She didn't mindlessly watch her life flow by; she thought seriously about its meaning.

Second, she kept God's word. What does this mean to us today? How should we do the same? Mary was attuned to reality. We, on the other hand, spend hours agonizing over alternatives to reality. Facts such as "I'm pregnant," "It's snowing outside," "The bank account is overdrawn," "My diagnosis is cancer," can't be endlessly discussed or contradicted. They are reality, and that is that.

Mary would accept the reality as coming from God's hand, designed for some mysterious but wonderful good. In contrast, we often waste our energies on "what might have been," spending precious time in Fantasyland when we should be facing What Is. Mary's discussion with the angel at the Annunciation is a model of brevity. By the time she gets to Elizabeth's home, she's over the shock and rejoicing.

An intelligent apprentice doesn't argue with the master — unless he or she wants to lose the job. Instead, a wise learner observes what materials, tools and techniques the senior craftsperson uses. If the observation is astute, the skills eventually transfer. Gradually, the master gives the apprentice more and more opportunities to practice.

But the teacher's effectiveness is stalled by a quarrelsome student who intrudes with questions like, "Why are you doing it *this* way? Shouldn't you do it *that* way?" Only the most patient practitioner would put up with such tedious interruptions. If we apply the analogy to God, it's clear that we often complain, suggest alternatives to the divine plan, and divert a clear, logical learning. When we think we know better, God must toss God's hands in frustration.

Maybe that's why God was so grateful when Mary came along. Finally, a human being who *got* it. She didn't second-guess, whine, balk, or offer a better idea. (For instance, "wouldn't Your son have more credibility if he were born to married, wealthy parents who could give him a good education?" "Surely You can do better than a *barn* for the birth of the Great Lord of all the universe?" "Was crucifixion really necessary? Couldn't You accomplish the same thing less painfully?") She must have figured, "If this is how God wants to do it, I'll cooperate. The only door into the future is trust."

Some of the people we most admire are those we call "at home in the world." They aren't constantly chafing, wanting something better; they're happy with what's happening right now. They don't drive themselves or others relentlessly because they have a gift of inner peace. Such qualities must have lodged squarely and amply in Mary.

Any young woman who becomes pregnant gets a quick course in trust. She doesn't understand the processes evolving within her, and worrying whether the baby is healthy doesn't help much. All she can do is give herself over to the wisdom of the body and time. It seems a bit odd when people compliment parents on the new baby's good looks, since their role is relatively minor. The miraculous creation and formation is God's.

Wise mothers learn quickly that the health and safety of the infant is beyond their control. Sudden infant death syndrome and other tragedies are largely unpreventable. The life that is most precious is also most vulnerable. While some parents try unsuccessfully to erect a defense shield, most learn that they cannot prevent disease, accident, or death. Just as in pregnancy, the life of the child rests more in God's hands than in theirs.

If this is true for all human beings, how much more it must have been true for Mary. The circumstances of Jesus' birth were precarious; the Bethlehem crib, while a precious image, was far less sanitary than hospital labor and delivery rooms today. The nursery would have been primitive at best, and there were no immunizations. Forced into exile early in the child's life, the little family had no passport to security in Egypt.

Mary must have moved through those early years on the strength of her trust. Just as air provides us with the oxygen we need to live, or water cushions us in a pool, so she must have relied on an enveloping sense of God's presence.

And trust was a two-way street. As an infinitely vulnerable infant, God incarnate relied on Mary for nurture, sustenance, protection, life itself. Although forced into difficult situations Mary probably wouldn't have chosen herself, she did not disappoint God.

Later in Jesus' life that dynamic continued: he seemed to search for a few people who trusted him, whom he could in turn trust. Sadly, only a handful seemed to fulfill that desire, and Mary headed the list. First and foremost, she gave him the trust he needed as much as milk or bread.

He in turn entrusted her with even the most difficult aspects of his life on earth. He asked her to understand why he had to leave the security of home, wander the roads preaching, seemingly deny her request at Cana, appear to have abandoned her, and die such an excruciating death that it must have wrenched her heart. That must be the ultimate trust: to ask someone we love to share our heartbreak.

Without apology or even much verbalization, Jesus told Mary: "This is how it must happen, and this is how it must end. Come with me faithfully, as you have from the very beginning."

Questions for Discussion or Reflection

- Have you ever been tempted to second-guess God, or offer God a better plan for your life?
- What were the circumstances?
- What was the outcome?
- How might Mary have acted in similar circumstances?

Mary as Mirror

Two biblical quotations inspire the image of Mary as mirror:

She is a reflection of eternal light, a spotless mirror of the working of God and an image of God's good news.
(Prov. 8:26)

God has shone in our hearts to give the light of the knowledge of God's glory in the face of Christ.
(2 Cor. 4:6)

What does the mirror image mean for one who looked directly into the face of Christ her son? Did she recognize there something of herself, a trait like her coloring or her smile? Did she see there God's glory? The human and divine, mingled in the face of Christ, must have had a special clarity for Mary, who looked at his face so often.

We understand their special relationship by looking around us at similar relationships. After I'd been friends with Carla for years, I finally met her daughter. Carla and I lived in different states, but we always got together when we were attending the same conventions or traveling to the same areas. Our friendship flourished via e-mail, and although I'd seen pictures of her daughter's wedding, I'd never met the Real Thing.

Until one day when I was in Carla's hometown and she invited me to dinner. We ate chili and drank margaritas on her deck, surrounded by candles and warm autumn breezes. For the first time, I got to know Carla's husband and her daughter, Claire. In the course of the evening, Claire's personality gradually emerged. Outgoing, funny, as personable as her mom, she was quick to compliment her mother's cooking or earrings.

Yet she was still her own person, a lively teacher beloved by her fifth graders. (I suspected the little boys had crushes on Claire.) I'd known her mother only as a mature woman; this delightful young adult gave me a glimpse of Carla's girlhood.

My older daughter and I have given many mother-daughter retreats where we've had informal chances to observe this special relationship. The pride the two take in each other is palpable. We delight in observing similar mannerisms, speech patterns, personality traits, and physical appearances. Through many years and different groups, one theme remains constant: mothers and daughters are always beautiful to each other, mirroring each other. The family traits are passed on like heirlooms, which gives us a perfect image for God's relationship with Mary and ours with her.

She mirrors God; we in turn mirror Mary. Think of a mother-daughter relationship without any disappointments, frustrations, or failures that could tarnish the intrinsic love and fidelity between the two. Subtract anxiety that daughter will repeat mother's mistakes. Delete daughter's embarrassment over mom's wardrobe or lack of tact.

Or enlarge the best mother-daughter relationship you know. Embroider it with all the best traits humans have. Starting with the finest we know of the human, imagine the divine. Now you've got a glimpse of Mary.

If she is the Monet painting, we're the initial sketch. If she's the exquisite Mary Oliver poem, we're the rough draft. We may have a long way to go, but we're placed on the same continuum. Some of us have further to go; others bear her qualities as surely as daughter mirrors mother.

In the closing cantos of *The Divine Comedy,* Dante captures this mirroring trait, describing Mary:

> Look now upon the face that is most like
> the face of Christ, for only through its brightness
> can you prepare your vision to see him.

Looking into Mary's mirror, we see what we most need. If we're Japanese or Polish, so is she. If we have lost a child, so has she. If we struggle to keep our commitments, so did she. If we face an unplanned pregnancy, she's been there. Yet as much as we identify with her, she refuses to be held hostage by any one group, nationality, or ideology. Her mirror is too large for constriction; she cannot be reduced to any narrow definition.

An editorial in *National Catholic Reporter* (October 26, 2007) calls for a return to the Mary who is "for all of us":

> Show us Mary of the Magnificat, a fierce mother who stands with the poor.... Give us Mary, protector of unwed mothers and those in difficult marriages, couples who give birth in poverty, those displaced by political rivalries, war, and violence, those who live in refugee camps.... Give us Mary, patroness of runaway children, the homeless, widows, and mothers who watch helplessly as their children are arrested, detained, tortured, and executed.
>
> Show us Mary, model of leadership in family and community, alert to pantries without enough food, the mentally ill, lepers, persons hurt by religious bigotry, and women destroyed by gender discrimination. Show us the Mary who will parent us to live as she did, focused on Jesus, following Jesus, doing what he told us to do when he preached the beatitudes and the corporal works of mercy as the full measure of our obedience to God.

Questions for Discussion or Reflection

- How do you respond to the image of Mary as mirroring God?

- How do you respond to the contemporary images of Mary in the final quotation from the *National Catholic Reporter*?

Mary, Feminine Face of God

During the years when patriarchy dominated the Christian church, people's yearning for the feminine reached toward Mary. That desire must have been even stronger when male dominance was more rigid and entrenched than it is today. Toward Mary people direct their deepest longings for that mysterious mix we call "feminine." Without stereotyping, we tend to ascribe certain traits to women: healing, tenderness, earthy directness, nurture, compassion, attentiveness to the small and vulnerable.

For the women who try to follow Christ, however devotedly, there is an undeniable gender gap. Much as we love him and try to live like him, that distance is still hard to bridge. I can ask a friend, brother, son, or husband how to be male, but it's still slightly distant. I'll never experience it directly. So too with Jesus.

The only way I know to be human is enfleshed as a woman. Mary closes that "gender gap" with God, showing us how to be fully, wholly, delightfully, exuberantly, *divinely* feminine.

Mary's apparitions, whether at Lourdes, Guadalupe, Zaragoza, Fatima, La Salette, Medjugorje, or Knock restore the feminine presence and highlight the balance between personal religious experience or testimony and public worship or official teaching. These appearances show the need for each new generation to have symbols particular to its time and place: whether roses, healing waters, jewels, stars, gate, dawn, or heavenly queen.

Mary opens a window for those who find their way to God through beauty, through women's incarnate experiences. Seekers like this find little resonance with abstractions or knowledge removed from daily life. But as Jim Forest writes, "Both the Son of God and His Mother are age-old archetypes, symbols by which the soul orients itself on its religious paths."[8]

Elizabeth Johnson adds: "In devotion to [Mary] as a compassionate mother who will not let one of her children be lost, what is actually being mediated is a most appealing experience of God."[9]

Question for Discussion or Reflection

♦ What is your favorite image of Mary? Use those listed in the fourth paragraph on page 37 as a starting point, or add your own.

Mary as Mentor

When I was a college junior, Carmen was a senior. The Indian caste system seems more flexible than the school hierarchy was then. Bizarre as it seems now, members of different classes rarely mingled. The Brahmins, or seniors, weren't cruel to younger students. They simply didn't notice their existence.

So I admired Carmen from afar. Because our college was small, juniors and seniors took the same seminars, where we often gave presentations. When it was Carmen's turn, I'd listen in awe of her style. Because she was from Cuba, her English was musical; her accent was lyrical. Her dark hair was always beautifully shaped; her gestures were poetic.

Although Carmen was oblivious to me, I looked to her with the uncritical admiration and pulsing insecurity of those whose identity is still wobbly. I aped her mannerisms. If our professor noticed that my presentations echoed Carmen's, she wisely refrained from comment.

The funny thing is that my obsession was so short-lived. I haven't thought about Carmen in forty years. I suppose I developed my own style and probably grew as oblivious as she was to younger people. At a convention where I'd spoken and signed books, I was genuinely shocked by an adolescent who approached gingerly and whispered, "I want to be you." "Oh no," I blurted, horrified. "You need to be *you.*"

Perhaps that last sentence contains the crux of modeling Mary. We honor her and place her template over our lives. But few of us are Jewish, none inhabit first-century Palestine, and most don't mother the Messiah. Where, then, are the connections?

It reminds me of my two daughters, who are ten years apart. When the younger one was growing up, she'd often repeat the same words as her older sister, do the same things, follow her everywhere. (Hence, I suppose, the stereotype of little sister as pest.) But eventually, older daughter went off to college and younger was left to her own devices.

It delighted me to watch her develop her own style, pursue interests that older sister didn't share, and eventually become her own person. They are still close, share many values, love reunions, and giggle on the phone a lot. (Hoorah for long-distance family calling plans.) But they have done what psychologists might call "individuation." They stand alone, each one unique and precious.

So too if we look to Mary as older sister, we hope to share many common qualities. In our early years the template was set: we aspire to model her. What is best about her is also what is best in us: nearness to Christ. The rest is a matter of style. God makes each of us as unique as snowflakes. The great creator, God rejoices in each one's special qualities.

Perhaps God looks on us as I do on my daughters, cherishing both the family resemblance and the individual traits. If Jesus is older brother, Mary is older sister. And God, seeing each of us says, "This is my beloved child, in whom I am well pleased." Maybe God's a gardener, equally delighted with daffodils, daisies, water lilies, and pansies.

In an era when we're sadly short of role models, Mary fills the bill. The rock stars, royalty, millionaires, and athletes held up for our admiration are often shallow. If we tried to follow them, we would find they starve the soul. With Mary, it's just the opposite. There's always more to admire and imitate.

Questions for Discussion or Reflection

◆ Have you ever been a mentor, or had a mentor?

◆ Based on that experience, how do you see Mary as mentor?

Vessel for God

When I was about thirteen, an insightful teacher gave me a book called *The Reed of God,* by Caryll Houselander. I don't remember whether I responded to the lyrical writing or the insights about Mary, but I resonated deeply with that book.

So I hesitated to reread Houselander over forty years later. Would I find her work unbearably sentimental, a mirror of my insecure, idealistic, yearning adolescent self? Would I be embarrassed by an antiquated view of Mary?

I was pleasantly surprised. The writing is still beautiful, and because it grew from the author's experience of the London blitz during World War II, realistic. Her theology is sound and hope-filled, because she holds out to all human beings the possibility of being like Mary, bringing Christ into our worlds.

What touched me most was Houselander's idea about the shape of our emptiness. This inner space is determined by the purpose for which we were created, the contemplation of God. Our inner spaces were designed for silence and solitude, but too often we clutter them with junk: noise, the satisfaction of trivial desires, the pursuit of fluff.

Or sometimes the overly serious fill the inner world with their causes. No matter how noble these are, they can block God's quiet entry.

We are all vessels for God, channels of God's presence and compassion to others. Houselander raises the question of what kind of containers we are. Mary was a reed on which God played music, a nest for an infant, and a chalice for the wine of sacrifice and gladness. Each image must undergo preparation for its purpose: the reed must be hollowed out and stops cut in it. A mother bird must gather twigs and other materials for a nest, then mold its roundness by shaping it to her breast. The gold of a chalice is gathered, melted, and beaten into shape.

In the process of molding a life, the initiative and the artistry is God's. Our task is to trust God's plan, and as Mary did, to receive a generous gift.

Houselander points out that Mary wasn't asked to renounce the world, enter a convent, or lead an army. To outward appearances her life didn't change much after the Annunciation: she continued to be a peasant woman and she carried out her plan to marry Joseph. As often happens when

God intersects human history, it's through ordinary people, not giant movers and shakers.

Mary models how we are to give our lives over to God, and through our unique affections, thoughts, and activities, bear Christ into our worlds. Just as he came into her body and used her flesh to develop as an infant, so he asks our hearts and hands to do his work on earth.

Because of Mary, then, no life is small or ordinary because every life is infused with the divine. Just as a pregnant woman is seldom conscious of the exact developments in her fetus, so we may not realize what work God is doing in us. But Mary offers hope that we might be transformed as she was.

Question for Reflection or Discussion

• Draw the kind of container that represents who you are now for God. Then draw one that shows the shape your life took in the past. Speculate on what kind of vessel you might become in the future.

Mary, Wise Fool

The poet Madeleine L'Engle describes this paradox:

> This is the irrational season
> When love blooms bright and wild.
> Had Mary been filled with reason,
> There'd have been no room for the child.

Most "wise," practical people would have listened politely to the angel's proposal and then just as politely said, "No thanks. I could never do it. Why not check with the girl next door?" Yet Mary mustered the inner gumption to say "yes." In doing so, she joined a long line of heroes who risked looking foolish. They stepped beyond the narrow borders of human esteem, valuing God's plan more than any that limited mortals could concoct.

Mary wasn't simply naïve. At the Annunciation she raised the question of her unmarried state because she knew the terrible societal cost. Even recently, the penalty for a woman having a child out of wedlock in parts of the Middle East has been burial alive or stoning. Our hopes that the twenty-first century is more enlightened may be unfounded. The fact that this punishment happens *now* gives us a glimpse of what the situation must have been *then!*

Our inner spaces were designed for silence and solitude, but too often we clutter them with junk: noise, the satisfaction of trivial desires, the pursuit of fluff.

Mary's response to the angel, "Fiat," or "let it be done to me" must have seemed reckless. Shouldn't she have qualified somehow? A more measured response would have been, "Let it be done as long as it doesn't hurt too much, ask too much, or damage those I love." But she was speaking to the God of Hannah, Sarah, Esther, and Miriam. So an unqualified "yes" was the only appropriate answer. Because she lived with the models of her foremothers, Mary could summon up their courage. Everything appeared to be against them, yet they trusted God and flourished. They were wise in the long run despite the short-term risk of appearing foolish.

The name "Maryam" means "to bear the bitterness of the time." Mary certainly was at the heart of the Hebrews' struggle for freedom. Just as Moses and Aaron's sister Miriam danced and played tambourines after the Hebrews escaped from Egypt (Exod. 15:20), Mary demonstrates how redemption and liberation go together. The wise woman doesn't mind appearing foolish, knowing that the final, saving word is God's. She knows how apparent tragedy can turn to treasure.

Question for Reflection or Discussion

+ Have you ever been in a situation where you or someone else *appeared* to act foolishly, when in fact you or they were acting wisely? Describe what happened and compare it to Mary's model.

Chapter Three _____

Mary around the World

A BOUT FIFTEEN YEARS AGO, a college president told the
parents of first-year students, "Your children will become citizens of the world. We don't even know what that
means yet, but we need to educate them for this role."
She went on to speak of foreign language immersion, study
abroad, international film fests, and many ways students
could interact with other cultures. The talk was prophetic.
Although parents today don't completely understand the dimensions of the world stage, we see our children becoming
better traveled, more fluent in other languages, and better
versed in other cultures than we ever were.

Even older people who grew up in a homogenized neighbor-
hood now have friends, colleagues, and acquaintances from
many nations and ethnic backgrounds. Conversations in grocery stores are a brew of many languages; people who were
once isolated now benefit from the rich mixture of many
cultures.

Perhaps Mary was the first citizen of the world and can
show us how to be better world citizens. All nations have
their representations of her, so she is Sudanese, Malaysian,
Brazilian, Canadian, French, Dutch: the United Nations in
one person. By looking at the way different cultures depict
her in their arts, we see her many nationalities.

In his book *Blessed Art Thou,* artist Michael O'Neill McGrath, O.S.F.S., painted Mary wearing both the Jewish prayer shawl and the Palestinian scarf, one on each shoulder. Dressed in black and white to show "the complementarity of opposites," she cradles in her arms a dove holding the olive branch of peace. Thus, she reconciles warring nations and hostile cultures. She teaches us how to disarm our hearts and abandon our resentments. This explains why one of her titles is "Queen of Peace."[10]

It would be impossible to cover adequately the world's many different representations of Mary and ways of honoring her. So this section will focus on a few examples that might suggest a small microcosm of the larger scene.

African Madonna

Into bizarre circumstances grace often makes entry. On a ranch in Wyoming designed for ecumenical renewal, I take a course from Esther De Waal, whose work on Celtic spirituality and Merton I have long admired. She has flown from her home on the border between Wales and England to a cowboy culture wilder than Hollywood could concoct. Into this rugged mountain scene she brings the orderly tradition of the Benedictine monastery. In log cabins we read and discuss the cloister of Canterbury cathedral. A constant theme in both cultures is reverence for Mary.

Her book *Lost in Wonder* also gives me an insight on Mary. The Latin *pondus,* Esther writes there, comes from *weigh:* "to hold something precious like a stone in the hand . . . letting it communicate its essence to us."[11] When Mary did not immediately understand, she pondered: a good lesson to those of us in the microwave generation, who want immediate answers and quick fixes.

At seventy-five, Esther believes that the only antidote to growing old is trying new things. So on the ranch, she rides a horse daily, something she hasn't done since she was fifteen. Her audacity pays tribute to the Benedictine motto "Always we begin again."

Esther also generously gives her time to private conversations outside of scheduled lectures. During one of our chats, I tell her about this book, which I'm drafting on a porch overlooking Ring Lake. The next day at lunch, Esther hands me a small package wrapped in a handkerchief. She explains that it has traveled around the world with her, and she thinks I might find it useful now. I almost race up the mountainside to my cabin, where I unwrap it gingerly.

Such gifts speak the exact word we need to hear precisely when we need to hear it. Within the handkerchief was a small brown statue, six inches tall, carved by Zimbabweans who care for AIDS orphans. That background may explain the apparent contradiction of a mother who holds her child tenderly, but at the same time, lets him go. It captures in wood what my words have failed to net: the tension in Mary between cradling and releasing, holding her child tight and giving him to the world. It is a tension we must all someday face. (See "The Art of Mothering" on page 94.)

In the motherhood department, I'm at a difficult juncture myself. For the first time in thirty-four years, all my children have left home. We remain close through phone and e-mail, and I'm delighted to receive calls from Manhattan, the ferry between Bainbridge Island and Seattle, Georgetown, or the University of North Carolina. We relish our times together

because they involve intensive coordination, synchronizing
schedules and buying plane tickets. We no longer meet casually over the washing machine or in the kitchen as we fill
the cereal bowls. Our times together are wonderful, but far
too infrequent.

Despite our efforts to stay connected, I still miss the children's warm familiar voices, the swirl of their activity, the
closeness of their bodies, their humor and energy filling the
house. I even miss their friends, who once seemed like an
intrusion — *more* noise, *more* cooking. Once I yearned for
quiet; now the house is far too still.

I look enviously at my friends who are grandmothers, who
balance toddlers in their laps at church. I even watch young
mothers interact with their children, trying to remember what
that phase was like. I recall a contradictory blend of wanting
to have those small people close to me always and longing to
regain my independence. I used to plead for one completed
sentence; now I write whole books!

Human beings have separated from their children for centuries. When God laments the Hebrew people, according
to the prophet Hosea, God speaks as though knowing this
sadness:

> When Israel was a child, I loved him,
> and out of Egypt I called my son...
> I led them with cords of human kindness,
> with bands of love,
> I was to them like those
> who lift infants to their cheeks.
> I bent down to them and fed them....
> How can I give you up, Ephraim?

How can I hand you over, O Israel?
My heart recoils within me;
my compassion grows warm and tender.
(Hos. 11:1, 4, 8)

We know in our heads that children must eventually lead their own lives, but some mother bear within us fights the separation. We want to hang on, trying to teach them one more thing, give them one more word of our profound wisdom, protect them from one more danger. So at this time, Mary has something unique to teach me, tailored to my present reality. She doesn't speak through words, but through the kindness of a teacher and the silent voice of a statue. My response to Mary, at a level beyond logical prose, emerges in poetry:

First I want to stroke her, tenderly,
slide my palm over the smooth wood grain,
draw a thumb down her profile,
brush her neck as I would
massage a friend in pain.

Baby face puckered,
the child sleeps in
a walnut-shaped oval,
a pear contour,
a cradle safe as womb.

Her broad hands hold
and release at once
because she knows the tension.
Carved into her peace, a sadness.
The weight of him in her arms, pondered.

Her terrible resignation to letting him go.
She will hold this body again, fractured,
flaccid. Pietà.

Mary in Spanish-Speaking Cultures

In the 350 years since her appearance, the Virgin of Guadalupe has been a central focus of Catholic worship in Mexico.
In *The Meeting of East and West,* F. S. C. Northrop writes
about the image hanging in every taxi and bus. Visitors to
the shrine in Mexico City are impressed by the devotion of
people who cross the huge square on their knees, approaching
the image with great reverence. Northrop believes that "nothing to be seen in Canada or Europe equals it in the volume or
the vitality of its moving quality or in the depth of its spirit
of religious devotion."

The origin of the image lies in the vision of Juan Diego,
a poor Aztec who had been converted to Christianity at the
age of fifty. He found in the new religion a spirit far different from the gods who demanded human sacrifice. In 1531,
Juan Diego encountered a lovely young woman surrounded
by golden light, who identified herself as Mary, Mother of
God. She asked that a church be erected at Tepeyac, a site that
reconciled the old and the new. Her appearance to Juan Diego
occurred at the same place where Tonatzin, Mother Goddess,
was once worshiped. Mary sent Juan to tell the bishop.

The Franciscan bishop asked for proof, which the Virgin
sent in the form of roses in December. When Juan Diego
opened his cape, the unseasonal flowers poured out and the
brightly colored image appeared on the *tilma,* or mantle. It

convinced the bishop, and hangs now in the basilica. The cactus cloth, which seldom lasts twenty years, shows no sign of decay and the colors remain bright. The millions who pray there find comfort in the maternal expression of the face and the dark shade of the skin. "She is brown, like us," one young Mexican-American asserts proudly.

Historians credit the miraculous picture with the conversion of 8 million native Americans between 1532 and 1538. Believers attribute many miracles to the glowing image. Surely Our Lady of Guadalupe speaks profoundly of the divine identification with the poor and the desire of the Holy One to participate in all humanity.

Her feast is celebrated with mariachi music, liturgies, dancing, meals, the retelling of the story, and an abundance of roses in December. Her shrine in Mexico City is the most popular one after the Vatican in the Catholic world.

From Latin America also comes a more recent image, the Madonna of the Street Children, guardian of children who are taken to brothels for tourists, who sniff glue to dull the pain of homelessness and hunger. But she consoles them. The girls are often named "Mary" in her honor.

Another startling image from Latin America is Madonna Leona, who rides naked on a lion. She stands in bold contrast to our "tamed" tradition! Unapologetic and powerful, she is a "woman who does not have to stifle the girl she once was." [12] Of course she comes from a long lineage: an ancient metaphor for God is the Lion of Judah.

Santiago Cortés-Sjöberg, a native of Zaragoza, Spain, where the Mary of the Pillar shrine is built, realizes that this depiction of Mary may be unknown to those who don't speak Spanish. But Mary has exercised a strong attraction for him ever since his boyhood. When he visited other Marian sites, they did not hold the same fascination. He concludes, "This relationship, into which you are born culturally, socially, and spiritually, can be so strong that 'your' Mary becomes even better than the 'other' Marys."

Knowing this might sound silly, he continues: "Devotion to Mary...cannot be dismissed just with psychological and sociological explanations.... It is something deeper and mysterious, something that transcends time, cultures and reason itself.... After all, faith is about love, mystery, and life. And all those are real, even if we cannot understand them."[13]

The United States: An Aging Mother

When our parish was remodeled, the new statue of Mary caused some controversy. Carved from wood, she is a rich chestnut color. However, some have protested because she is an older, peasant woman, seated in a position of strength. "The problem," our pastor observed, "is she's not *attractive*. What does that say about Mary — and all women — when we judge them by how pretty they are?"

Indeed, the United States has made a cult of youth and taken it to such an extreme that the most shallow, tedious starlet gets huge press simply because she's pretty. Substantive issues are pushed off the front page when Britney or Paris upstages them. It leaves those who are aging in a quandary. Once the elderly were respected for their wisdom; now they are dismissed as useless. Industries have mushroomed to reduce wrinkles, dye gray hair, and camouflage the natural marks of aging. Women who have shaped their identities around their appearance are flummoxed: if the taut body and beautiful face deteriorate, who am I?

Mary speaks powerfully to those who are losing the last vestiges of youthful grace, myself included. "Where did that old lady in the mirror come from?" I wonder often. Then Mary reminds us aging baby boomers: what's important isn't the appearance. What matters is within. Have we an inner peace that spills into love and generosity for others? Rather than get lost or sunk in nostalgic memories, we might follow the advice of St. Elizabeth Ann Seton.

In contrast to the popular literature about diminishment, Seton spoke joyfully of fulfillment in her later years. She was forty-eight and in poor health; she didn't have long to live. Two of her daughters had died young, but she didn't whine. Instead she wrote, "Look up! Be grateful for the good that yet remains."

While our parish statue of Mary is not a slender girl, she conveys a strength that only long experience can bring. Because of all she has endured, she invites confidence. Those who are hurting, or needing a grandmother's lap find a warm welcome in her.

The Celtic Mary

The ancient residents of the British Isles looked into their mirrors (or reflecting pools) and saw a Mary like themselves. We learn of her from the prayers and poems passed down in the oral tradition. The people were so easy and familiar with Mary that they interjected her name frequently in conversation ("Mary Mother!" or "O Mary of Grace!").

Esther De Waal writes in *The Celtic Vision:* "Mary, while still hailed as the Queen of Heaven, is also a woman to whom to confide about duties around the house, a woman who knew their sort of life since she herself had experienced simplicity, hardship, and tears."[14]

Their worldview did not divide spiritual and temporal, heavenly and earthly as more dualistic philosophies did. De Waal says, "There is no divide here between this world and the next. Heaven and earth are interconnected and interacting. So Mary is there at the start of the day when the peats have to be lifted from the hearth."[15]

The intimacy extended even to the lowliest chores, as Celtic people prayed: "Come, Mary, and milk my cow." "I will raise the hearth-fire as Mary would."[16] Irish sons and daughters emigrated abroad so often that the mother's blessing echoed Mary. Her son also left on a perilous journey that led eventually to his death.

Mary's feasts were ritually celebrated, and the people's songs would encompass a broad range between the glorious one, bright as the moon or sun, and the earthy mother who blesses the corn crop. One couplet that captures the great spectrum praises:

> Thou shining Mother of gentleness,
> Thou glorious Mother of the stars.[17]

An Asian Perspective

The website of the Asian Christian Art Association gives a new perspective on Mary as she appears to contemporary artists in Korea, China, and Indonesia. Kim Jae Im leaves faces blank to emphasize shapes: the tenderness with which Gabriel bends over Mary, or her attentiveness, listening to the angel's message. In another painting, Mary dances her child into the world to the music of a Korean drum. She holds her baby tightly but her feet appear to jig.

He Chi uses brilliant color and shapes that recall stained glass, but his Chinese art is totally different from what we would expect to see at Chartres or Canterbury. In *Annunciation* Mary appears to be playing a flute, while the traditional lilies still bloom at her feet. In *Escape to Egypt*, Jesus with a tuft of black hair is held in the "happy baby" yoga posture, while the triangle of an Egyptian pyramid looms behind the family.

In *The Annunciation* by Hari Santosa of Indonesia, Mary looks Balinese, with a flower in her hair, large hoop earrings, and a striped skirt. The angel is part of a swirl of sky, wind, jungle, and birds. Muted brown, avocado, and bronze tones contrast with the primary colors used by He Chi.

Woman for All Nations

We who have grown accustomed to the Mary of Western art, in her blue robe with her plump, pink baby, do well to step outside our usual view and appreciate her in kimono or sari, her child with coal black hair reaching for an apple, butterfly, or water gourd. Perhaps this broader view prepares us to better see Mary everywhere — as Father Andrew Greeley once did, on a bus in Chicago, in a mom juggling baby and Christmas presents. When Father Greeley offered to hold the packages, she smiled with what he terms an unmistakable

Madonna luminosity, which keeps the world on course and the universe in tune.

In Russia, art depicts Mary as bringing home Adam. As one scholar comments, "She tells us the world isn't just the disastrous stage of an absurd tragedy.... It is a place for the hope that protects life and makes the improbable thing that we call compassion come true."[18]

We who have grown accustomed to the Mary of Western art, in her blue robe with her plump, pink baby, do well to step outside our usual view and appreciate her in kimono or sari, her child with coal black hair reaching for an apple, butterfly, or water gourd.

In *Blessed Art Thou,* the book mentioned earlier, Michael O'Neill McGrath shows Mary in a variety of settings that blend cultures and disrupt stereotypes. To depict the title *Queen of Angels,* for instance, he paints a jazz band of angelic musicians playing banjo, horn, and bongo drums to accompany the Magnificat. A dark-skinned Mary wears a flower over one ear, Hawaiian style. She wears her hair in African braids — a blessed relief from the pasty white, blue-eyed blonde Marys of my childhood. She is much more interesting and vibrant because she combines the richness of different cultures, like a festival of many nations.

According to Acts 1:14, Mary was present when the Holy Spirit filled Jesus' followers on the day of Pentecost. At that time "Jews from every nation under heaven" were gathered in Jerusalem. Amazed, they heard the disciples speaking in their native languages, about "God's deeds of power" (Acts 2:11). Through the Holy Spirit's presence, the language barrier vanished, and people from all nations became as one. How appropriate that in Mary this miracle continues. Through her, animosities disappear and warring children make peace in one mother.

Questions for Discussion or Reflection

+ What is your ethnic background?

+ Is your image of Mary shaped by it?

+ How do you feel about representations of Mary from other cultures?

+ Do you agree that within her lies an answer to global warfare, a recognition of our common humanity?

She Who Holds the Tension

MARIAN SHRINES STRETCH from Lourdes in France to Walshingham in England to Guadalupe in Mexico and Medjugorje in the former Yugoslavia. They are a tribute to universal admiration of this woman, yet it's a stretch to imagine Mary among us, on the subway or in the big box store of the twenty-first-century United States. We wonder how to connect her more closely to our lives.

She transcends nationalities, yet every culture has its favorite representations of her. Mary is revered by Muslims, who mention her thirty-four times in the Koran, and various kinds of Christians. Her son opposed killing, yet Mary's image was carried on banners by the Crusaders' armies. Liberals like her gutsiness; conservatives emphasize her compliance. In the United States, proponents of women's ordination turn to Mary as the model of a priestly person who brought Christ into the world. But other cultures uphold her more traditional, passive role.

This overview only scratches the surface of the tensions surrounding Mary. Her life itself was filled with them, so when we admire her tranquility, we forget that she is like the duck gliding serenely on the water's surface, paddling like crazy underneath. The joke is told of the exhausted mother, dragging her many disheveled children to church. There, a young priest exalted the Blessed Mother, pointing to her serene statue, far beyond this world's chaos. "Yeah," harrumphed the frazzled mom: "Her and her *one*."

The joke is humorous and understandable, given the aloof way Mary has been presented. But that kind of distancing does a disservice to a woman who bore a lioness's share of hardship, carrying tensions throughout her life — and beyond.

During Mary's Life

Most young women would be baffled and overwhelmed by the news Gabriel brings. Mary probably was too — at first. She felt like anyone whose plans have been disrupted and whose life has changed suddenly and dramatically.

But after time to get used to the idea of being an unwed mother and a reassuring journey to her cousin Elizabeth, Mary breaks into a song of praise. The older woman must give her the affirmation and security she needs. With that encouragement, she mines her tradition for suitable words to wrap around the new event.

Proclaiming the Magnificat, Mary stands as a link between the Old and New Testaments. She uses the language of the Old (her foremother Hannah's song) while welcoming the new, Jesus. Later scholars would call her "the new Eve," who reverses the mistake made in the garden of Eden. She shows us how to stand on wobbly thresholds or make precarious transitions into the unknown.

Instead of cursing our insecurity at such times, we should model Mary's grateful exuberance. The French poet Jean Mambrino, S.J., suggests that the only hours lost or wasted are those when we forget to praise.[19] It must have been tempting for Mary to worry and fret, as it often is for us. Instead, she shows us another way to respond to the unknown: joyful trust in whatever God sends. Thus, in a wintry process, the hard bulb of anxiety flowers into crocus.

Stressful situations would continue throughout her life: fleeing into the unfamiliar land of Egypt; losing Jesus in the temple, then hearing the odd explanation for his absence; nursing Joseph through his final illness; trying to understand the mysterious message of John the Baptist and his terrible beheading; puzzling through Jesus' initial dismissal at Cana; seeing her son's public ministry draw him away from her; hearing him "cut the ties" as he proclaimed that every follower was as close as his mother.

Ronald Rohlheiser gives a fine explanation of the tension Mary carried at Calvary. In a long descending spiral, humans passed along to others the evils they had experienced. If their child was killed in war, they'd retaliate by murdering the enemy. If their house was destroyed, they'd seek revenge on the destroyer.

Yet Mary and Jesus put a stop to that. They didn't "pay back" the cruel torture, the agonizing climb to Calvary, the painful nails of crucifixion. The evil stopped with them; they refused to pass it along. Mary suffers the worst with true strength. Hers is the ultimately victorious stance of the oppressed.

After the deaths of many charismatic religious figures, their followers descended into arguments over how to carry out the mission and embody the vision. St. Francis experienced the dissent even before his death; it seemed to be a pattern for other leaders.

So it is likely that, being human, the early Christians disagreed on how to continue Jesus' work. Paul records the argument over circumcision; we can only speculate about other squabbles.

It must have been tempting for Mary to worry and fret, as it often is for us. Instead, she shows us another way to respond to the unknown: joyful trust in whatever God sends. Thus, in a wintry process, the hard bulb of anxiety flowers into crocus.

In the midst of this stood Mary. We know how much she missed her son and loved his friends. To see them fighting must have broken her heart. There is no record in Scripture about how she handled tensions as the Christian community grew, but from previous accounts we can guess that her approach continued much the same. She must have taken these struggles to prayer as she had all the others, "pondering them in her heart."

After Mary's Death

Later, as the theology of Mary developed, she was still caught in the tension: between what the doctrines proclaimed and what the people believed, between church leadership and simpler folk. Many pagans converting to Christianity in the late fourth century transferred to Mary their former devotion to the goddess Isis. Art historians show the parallels between this woman with the baby god-king Horus on her lap and the image of Madonna and Child. In 431, the Council of Ephesus gave Mary the title Mother of God, which as religious historian Karen Armstrong comments, gave her "celebrity" status.

From the fifth century on, Marian feasts coincided with the traditional natural cycle. Mid-May sowing celebrated her queenship; mid-August harvest brought the feast of her Assumption, and the winter solstice, or birth of the sun, came near Christmas. For the common people, Mary was patron of fertility, the earth mother who helped with conception and birth, assured rain and good crops.

The origin of the Black Madonna lies in this belief, not necessarily in cultures where people's skin was black. These dark statues were carried in procession so people could hold up their sick children to her. Her large peasant hands blessed the harvest, because as a peasant herself, Mary understood the importance of such earthy realities. Meanwhile, religious officials debated whether Mary's hymen was broken in childbirth and whether she remained perpetually a virgin.

During the Middle Ages, Mary's image fit the structure of feudal society. She became the royal mistress of the heavenly court. Crusaders plunged into battle believing they honored Mary, their queen. In the twelfth through the fifteenth centuries, Mary's glory grew "ever brighter in inverse proportion to the downgrading of real women."[20] As the movement toward a celibate clergy got under way, physical sexuality was rejected, so the spiritualizing of Mary's motherhood became a natural consequence.[21]

Mary was the arena for tension again during the Protestant Reformation, with Catholics boosting devotion at the Council of Trent and reformers protesting that belief was moving too far from a scriptural basis. As Christ grew less human, more the stern judge, people turned to Mary for mercy. If God was feared, then Mary was trusted. (How she must have hated this split between her son and herself!)

In 1858, a fourteen-year-old girl named Bernadette saw Mary near Lourdes, France. Today, millions of pilgrims still visit her shrine there, seeking healing. In 1917, Mary appeared to children in Fatima, Portugal, bringing a message of peace. While theologians hesitate to endorse Marian apparitions, the people reject their "scientific" approach. Mary remains a warm, maternal archetype who draws them regardless of official teaching. A deep emotional need for her seems to surface especially when the world is insecure or hostile. She offsets people's fears and gives them shelter, just as our own mothers would.

Throughout history, one can see a tension between popular devotion to Mary and the institution's restraint, or between the warm, affective domain and the cooler, more thoughtful definition of dogmas. Into the first group fall symbols and images such as the Queen of Angels, the Mystical Rose, the Seat of Heaven, the Star of the Sea, Our Lady of Bons Secours, the Gate of Heaven, the Morning Star.

The formal Marian doctrines are the Immaculate Conception and the Assumption, both declared because of popular demand. Somehow one merges into the other: the doctrinal statements get turned into songs, artwork, and feasts. The doctrine inspires the popular expression; the popular expression gives flesh to the doctrine.

Even within the Catholic Church, the pendulum has swung between lows and highs of Marian devotion. In relatively recent times, the Second Vatican Council said, deferring to the ecumenical movement: "We encourage Catholics to foster a loving devotion for Mary as our custom has been for so many centuries.... But at the same time ... we should all be careful not to act in such a way that others will misunderstand us, especially other Christian Churches that might not foster such a strong devotion to Mary."[22]

Then Pope John Paul II reversed that trend with an intense devotion to Mary. He named her Co-Redemptrix, which puzzled some Catholic theologians and alienated some other Christian traditions. Now some Protestants are "rediscovering" Mary, and songs honoring her are published in their hymnals.

Perhaps the greatest tension springs from the difference between a young peasant woman in an obscure outpost of the Roman Empire and the extraordinary worldwide movement she inspired. Jaroslav Pelikan, author of *Mary through the Centuries,* writes, "You could copy on an eight-and-a-half-by-eleven sheet everything there is about Mary in the New Testament.... To get from such skimpy evidence to what she has become is an astonishing example of how an idea can develop out of small beginnings."[23] Or perhaps it's a tribute to the power of grace and human affection.

Contemporary Metaphor: A Posture of Praise

An image for Mary comes to me during yoga class. In front of me is a beautiful Jewish woman named Leigh, who moves with the grace of the professional dancer she is. As we slide into a particularly difficult stretch, I worry about doing a combination of standing and kneeling. Leigh not only achieves *that;* she also lifts her arms wide and throws her head back. It is a joyous stance of greeting the morning, open to whatever the day brings.

As I silently admire Leigh's beauty and grace, I find myself, oddly enough, able to assume the same posture. The mirror presents a startling image: klutsy *moi*, stretching proudly, arms extending in that sweeping gesture of welcome. Because I've been somewhat saturated in reading and thinking about Mary, it occurs to me: just as I model Leigh, we are all called to model Mary.

We tend to think that the tensions we carry are uniquely ours; no one else could possibly understand. That's where Mary comes in. The tensions during and after her life, described above, spring from that curious nature we all bear, the mingling of human and divine.

Madeleine L'Engle explains that it is impossible for us to understand what it means to be God's children. Rarely do we introduce ourselves as God's daughter or son; seldom do we think of others, even those we love, this way.

Yet, L'Engle says, Jesus came to teach us, "to live with us for a few years to show us what we ought to be and could be. Christ came to us as Jesus of Nazareth, wholly human and wholly divine, to show us what it means to be made in God's image."[24]

If we think we could never achieve that sublime nature he demonstrated, Mary shows us that it *is* possible. She lived that way herself. One like us achieved the balanced stance. One who carried terrible tensions turned difficulties to praise. When we try even slightly to follow her, it places us on a larger stage, beyond our personal trivia. It challenges us to think of ourselves in radically creative and powerful ways, as daughters and sons of Mary.

Questions for Discussion or Reflection

• What tensions do you face now?

• What might Mary say if you turned to her for help with these?

———————————————————————

Chapter Five

The Earlier Triptych: Annunciation, Visitation, Birth of Jesus

W HILE THREE EVENTS have already been covered briefly in "Mary for All Seasons," they seem so pivotal to her life that they deserve a chapter to themselves: the Annunciation, the Visitation and the Birth of Jesus.

Annunciation

Into most lives comes an experience so profound we never forget it. Whether for good or evil, it shapes us and makes an indelible mark. For Mary it was the Annunciation. Something must have prepared her to answer as easily as she did, "I am the servant of the Lord." She was intimate with God, attuned to God's presence. She knew the religious tradition of her people; she also knew their powerlessness under Roman rule. So she gave God her vulnerability, her inner peace. It was enough: she was suddenly transformed from "servant" to "highly favored one."

Whenever she grew doubtful, tired, or frightened, she must have looked back on that turning point, that mysterious experience of a calling far beyond herself or anything she could dream. In "Annunciation," the poet Denise Levertov offers a new angle on Mary's character: "but we are told of meek obedience. No one mentions / courage."[25]

Mary's response to Gabriel at the Annunciation seems central to understanding her. It's the beginning of her public story, crucial to her identity. It's also the moment in her life that most commentators have dissected endlessly. Finding a new angle on that famous "fiat" ("be it done to me as you have said") is probably impossible, so this chapter will look at the background, then the Annunciation in terms of some metaphors, finally its applications to us today.

Background: A Parallel Tension

Sometimes we think we've got a monopoly on stress. Then we consider Mary. On one hand, she was steeped in the Torah and had memorized sections of it since she probably couldn't read. Almost through her veins coursed the story of God's fidelity to God's people. She would have lit the Sabbath candle each week as a graphic reminder of God's goodness. She would have sung the psalms regularly.

Couldn't God have disabled Herod with a simple lightning bolt or aneurism, sparing this small, besieged family an arduous trip with a young child?

On the other hand, she lived under Roman oppression. She had friends who were sold into slavery with their children when Romans slaughtered two thousand men of her country.

As if being caught between those two powerful forces wasn't enough, she receives a most puzzling message, which must have made her think, "Why me?" Her conversation with the angel is brief, but it turns her life cattywampus. Afterward, she must have repeated and weighed the words, trying to remember every tone and nuance. Yet, as much as she tried to understand, the angel didn't give her an agenda. She has no script for what to expect after the startling visit.

Her dilemma is like ours. We move between two worlds: the promises of our faith, the sad realities of our culture. We place our hopes in the former, yet we also know the tragedies and disasters that can leave intelligent people doubting whether God has any stake at all in our world. If we take comfort in our faith, we're accused of ignoring reality. If we focus only on people's inhumanity, we risk despair.

Those of us audacious enough to explore this chapter of Mary's story wonder why God's sense of timing seems to be so badly off. Couldn't the news of the pregnancy have waited until she was safely, respectably married to Joseph? Couldn't the birth have come when they were comfortably settled at home, with a "support system" of friends and relatives cushioning the harshness for a young girl? If God *really* loved the mother of Jesus so much, why put her through such shame, embarrassment, and upheaval? Couldn't God have disabled Herod with a simple lightning bolt or aneurism, sparing this small, besieged family an arduous trip with a young child?

Mary's son would later cure blindness, and to some extent all human beings are blind. Since we can't see beyond the present, we balk at hardship and inconvenience, unaware why they are so necessary. When tragedy strikes, we struggle to believe that it comes from God's hand and ask a question like the one above: If God loves us as we're so often told, why must we suffer so much?

Ladislas Orsy, S.J., a professor at Georgetown Law center, speaks of human hopes, which define expectations for the future and then cling to them tenaciously. Divine hope, on the other hand, means immersion in God's plan. "God guarantees a good outcome but without telling us what it will be." So Mary agreed to a plan she didn't know and couldn't direct. "Her participation . . . was perfect; she never said, 'I had hoped.' "[26]

Although she participated actively in her own drama, Mary apparently didn't question the way it unfolded. She simply proceeded, one step at a time, as we all do, into mystery. While she didn't try to hide her fear or puzzlement, she also knew the remedy for our human failure to see: blind trust. At one of her most confused and troubled times, shortly after the angel's disruptive message, she poured out praise. The God of her foremothers had been consistently faithful to a people who never quite deserved such abundance. Surely God's nature hadn't changed but rather remained the bedrock for her belief.

Throughout history, other great women have found themselves plunked squarely into dilemmas as painful as Mary's. They, too, discovered ways to keep trusting God against all the evidence. Consider, for instance, the nineteenth-century reformer Josephine Butler, who after the tragic death of her small daughter became an advocate for young women in Oxford. After being seduced by older married men, they were often abandoned, pregnant. Most remarkable about the story is Josephine's resolve not to demonize the thoughtless men.

Another example, Etty Hillesum, a Jewish mystic who died at Auschwitz, walked the same razor's edge between deep prayer and the atrocities around her. Her soul became a battleground between two forces: On one hand, she vowed to avoid denial, to name exactly what was happening. On the other hand, she resolved not to be angry or hateful. If the Nazis were merciless, she must be merciful. Her remarkable achievement, forgiving the unforgivable, is recorded in her autobiography, *An Interrupted Life*. When Etty was ultimately transported to the death camp, she vowed to be the "thinking heart of the barracks."

In a similar situation, Mary became the reflective pulse of the Roman Empire. Her contribution to humanity far outweighed the army's brutal conquests around the known world. In the long run, the oppressors would not be victorious. They would one day kill her son, but he would rise. He would unfurl a banner of hope for all oppressed peoples. Just as she would predict in the Magnificat, the loud voices of power don't have the final say.

Because Mary understood the kind of tensions we face, she can help us here. She lived with the dramatic contrasts, made her peace with disparate worlds. Throughout her life, she would help her friends remember the stories of God's saving encounters with humankind, especially through her son. When the little community of Jesus' followers leaned toward despair, she whispered the good news. She directed their sights toward hope.

We too must live on hope, based not on any human outcome but on trust in God's promise. We are baptized into the same gift of faith that Mary had. We have been invited to participate in the fullness of God's life just as she was. We too are asked to look into Jesus' face and birth Christ into our worlds.

Metaphors

As dawn comes to the Rockies, I'm poised in a lookout between the rising sun to the east and the pink-tinged mountains to the west. The dawning process reminds me of Mary. The sun rises slow and stately, gradually gilding each pine needle, tinting the rock formations. In those radiant moments, I know why the early settlers called this range Sangre de Cristo, or blood of Christ.

God orchestrates our lives as God does the fiery symphony playing out here. How do we respond? Mary answered perfectly, every harp string attuned, every fiber of her being singing "yes." She echoed that first creation, where God said "let there be light," and everything God called came precisely into being as God envisioned. If any human gets it right, Mary does. Her soul magnified the Lord just as the rock formations redden, reflecting the sun. (In the afternoon, we call this phenomenon "alpenglow.")

How do we model her? Perhaps a homey analogy shows the way. It isn't meant to be irreverent, but to show Mary's proximity to the things of daily life. Just as the Celtic oral tradition asked her to be part of beer-making or bread-baking, so we can invite her into our ordinary routines. Hence, the "muffin analogy."

I'm fond of blueberry muffins. Sometimes apple cinnamon or banana nut look intriguing, but I have my loyalties. Often, rushed, in an airport, hotel, or coffee shop, I'll buy one that's a disappointment. The only three blueberries are all arranged on top, so the rest is a sorry, bland blob of white flour and sugar. Or the muffin is encased in plastic and was probably baked three months before and three thousand miles away.

Despite these frustrations, I continue hopeful, trying them out in various strange forms.

One morning, the perfect configuration of events occurred. Blueberries had gone on sale at the local grocery store, and a five-pound box dominated the refrigerator. It was a Saturday, so I had a little more time than usual. Friends were coming for dinner — a perfect excuse to make blueberry muffins. So I did, with a *lot* of blueberries, whole wheat flour, and TLC. No plastic was involved in their production. They oozed their sweet purple juices and filled the house with fragrance. I baked early that July day, because temperatures were predicted to hit 100 and I didn't want the oven to contribute any more heat later in the afternoon.

No one was home, so no one would witness me snitching an early sample. Proudly, I took my muffin to the deck with coffee and reveled in the green surrounding me.

Whenever I eat another blueberry muffin, I'll compare it to that one. It came as close to perfection as anything on this earth ever does. Bird song, summer warmth, the anticipation of friends for dinner may all have contributed to the experience and may shape that scene in memory. On a frigid winter morning, I'll remember and say, "Ah, *that* was the best blueberry muffin!" It raised the bar for every one to follow.

Comparing Mary to a muffin may be a special brand of heresy as yet unnamed, so remember: you saw it here first. But perhaps it's not such a stretch. God, delighting in Mary, saw the epitome of humanity. Did God smile with pride, rejoicing in her as she rejoiced in God? Do all human beings contain some spark of Mary that endears them to their creator? When we act generously or kindly, does God see our resemblance to Mary? The Greek stoic philosopher Epictetus wrote, "You bear God within you, poor wretch, and know it not." Mary turned that situation around: she bore God within, clearly and knowingly. Her "yes" may be the hinge in a string of actions whereby her great-great-grandchildren follow Mary's footsteps.

Seeding for Abundance

How was it for you, Mary?
Finding in the angel's eyes
a light you would see later,
looking into your son's face.

The words sing like bells or
drops falling into a still lake.
She has the quiet to receive
them, peace of green meadow.

And what a flowering then!
She blossoms as we would later,
echoing her "yes" in many
languages, inflections, songs.

No accident that gardens and
wildflowers bear her name.
Mystic rose, garlands of
stained glass, life's profusion.

Questions for Discussion or Reflection

• What do you think Mary did with the anger she must have felt at Roman oppression of her people?

• How do you handle your anger at oppressive systems today?

- How did Mary find balance between the promise of her faith tradition and the evidence all around her of brutal injustice?

- How was she quiet enough internally to receive the angel's word?

- How do you achieve the same peace?

- How did Mary handle her fears?

- How can she help you deal with yours?

Visitation

Luke makes Mary an active participant in the Annunciation, an agent cooperating with God in the redemption of humanity. God continues to act through her at the Visitation. In the warmth of Elizabeth's acceptance, away from the small-town gossip of home, Mary breaks forth into a song that looks back and forward. It celebrates her ancestor Hannah and promises a wonderful justice to come.

Mary and Elizabeth could be two soccer moms, comparing notes on the sidelines, or two relatives chatting on the porch. The scene begins in an ordinary encounter, family members having a reunion. But then the meeting creates fireworks. German theologian Dietrich Bonhoeffer, who died in a Nazi camp, calls Mary's Magnificat "the most passionate, the wildest, one might even say the most revolutionary Advent hymn ever sung . . . a hard, strong, inexorable song about collapsing thrones and humbled lords of this world, about the power of God and the powerlessness of humankind."[27]

Despite a long tradition (which continues today) of women looking to men for support and affirmation, here, as theologian Susan Ross points out, they find it in each other. One reason Elizabeth may praise Mary so exuberantly is that she has spent six months with a silent husband. Perhaps she has isolated herself from neighbors who mock her pregnancy in old age. Whatever the reason, her blessing pours forth from a long silence with heightened velocity.

Neither woman exalts herself; they rejoice in God's goodness to them. Luke gives us a cameo scene of their first encounter; we can only speculate how their conversation continued during the next three months. They probably returned to the same themes, just as close friends delight in retelling the same stories, embellishing with details. If we were able to hide a recording device in that home, we might find on it a symphony of praise.

When Mary leaves Elizabeth's home, both women still face enormous challenges. Mary is young, unmarried. Her cousin is old, with a husband who is, at best, puzzled. Both live in small towns prone to gossip. They know that something is unusual about their sons, but they haven't begun to plumb those mysteries. Yet we can intuit that both feel more empowered, confident, encouraged to confront what's ahead because they have experienced deep affirmation, grounded in each other.

Two Cousins Meet

The richness stirring in her
overflows; she cannot contain
the mixed emotions. Gangly,
young girl energy poured into

the journey, the loping impulse,
the questions carried to Elizabeth.

Mary well met in the Judean hills.
The welcome there, a glowing.
Women who have long loved
each other, now with new loves,
the children within. Mary reassured,
her unspoken questions answered
by the dance of a tiny John.

Questions for Discussion or Reflection

- Write your own poem, song, or dance of joy. How do you give praise?

- How do you participate in the universal work of praising God's goodness?

Birth of Jesus

Again we confront such a wealth of resources, it's hard to choose what might mean the most. So we ask, of all the material on the nativity and Mary's role in it, what would have the most relevance to contemporary people? We still yearn for the simplicity and pure love of the mother and child. Father Andrew Greeley writes, "God loves us both like a father and a mother. And the Mary metaphor reflects this. The way that a mother loves a newborn child whom she's holding in her arms and is about to nurse — that's the way God loves us."[28]

We long for the security of a mother's arms. We also like our holidays cozy, predictable, sterilized of the scandal that plagued the first Christmas. Philip Yancey points out an interesting fact often overlooked in our usual celebration. It would have satisfied the Roman census for Joseph to have registered alone. Did he drag Mary along to spare her from nasty rumors, or fear that she might give birth alone in a hostile environment? "Nine months of awkward explanations, the lingering scent of scandal — it seems that God arranged the most humiliating circumstances possible for his entrance, as if to avoid any charge of favoritism."[29]

Or did Joseph, pure and simple, love Mary, and like many people who have strong feelings for each other, not want to be apart during uncertain times? Was she so vulnerable that he simply wanted to protect her? His attitude calls to mind those at both ends of the relationship spectrum: young lovers, thrilled with the discovery of each other, eager to touch, reluctant to be separated. While we are attracted to their lithe beauty, we also admire aging lovers: carefully guiding each other across dangerous parking lots or faithfully visiting the Alzheimer's facility even when one spouse no longer recognizes the other. Whatever Joseph's motive, he is a model of fidelity for spouses and dads today.

Since we are so familiar with the nativity story, we rarely consider alternate endings. What if Joseph had, like a good Jewish boy, doggedly and faithfully observed the law? According to the custom of the time, Mary would have been stoned in the public square. Lying in a pool of blood would be nothing but a small, limp bundle for her parents (if they weren't too ashamed) to carry away. But even before his dream, Joseph resolved to break with custom and "put Mary away privately."

That says something about Joseph, of course: his willingness to step beyond the law within which he'd been raised, to act from a larger sense of God's peculiar abundance. It also suggests that Mary was strong enough in her belief to convey it to Joseph. He couldn't dismiss her story, as most men of his day would, as a girl's fantasy. Instead, he believed her, hard as it must have been. She must have communicated powerfully — and we can only imagine the conversation they must have had!

What else does Christmas teach us today? The event was filled with surprises, which often knock us off balance. God apparently has a knack for sending us unexpected gifts that transform us into people we never dreamed we would be. The prophecy of Isaiah to Ahaz prefigures the birth of the Messiah. The prophet tells Ahaz that God will give him a baby as a sign (Isa. 7:9). Who was the "gift consultant" on that one? "What Ahaz needed, with Assyria breathing down his neck, was a good army, not a baby."[30]

It's humbling for modern, achievement-oriented sorts to admit that God doesn't necessarily want our talents and treasures, which eventually fade. "Mary offered only space, love, belief.... In the end, when all other human gifts have met their inevitable limitation, it is the recollected one, the bold virgin with a heart in love with God who makes a sanctuary of her life, who delivers Christ who then delivers us."[31]

A Jesuit priest writes that in a male-centered world, people may focus more on Jesus' coming than on his mother's concerns. She must have been filled with fear and confusion. He asks, "Do we give enough attention in our prayer and celebration to her interior life — this young woman called by forces she did not fully understand to give birth to a child whose coming was shrouded in so much mystery?"[32]

A prompt for prayer during this season asks what we long for, wait for, and hunger for. It asks further, "how does the image of the Christ child in his mother's arms speak to my hopes?"

My initial answer is that I want to become the kind of person Mary is, wrapping her arms around the newborn's potential as well as the adult son's corpse. To be that nurturing, she must be both strong and relaxed: nothing spooks the young more than a wimp or an uptight hypocrite. It takes a lot of quiet time and experience to become a welcoming home for anyone, especially the young who can tend to be prickly at times.

When my son was diagnosed with cancer at the age of thirty-four, shortly before Christmas, I turned to Mary. Here was a woman, like myself, who had gone through her son's surprising birth, life, and death. She'd shown the rest of us how to do it, gracefully, generously, with dignity and a calm centeredness. "We are not told that...Mary saw the angels or heard the *Gloria* in the air."[33] Instead, she spent that day in the homely atmosphere of a stable. One like myself, she must have answered our prayers for a cure: six months later, my son seems healed.

At Christmas Mary shows us how small, unexpected things can be holy; indeed, how through her and her son, all of human life is now spectacularly blessed.

Christmas

Hers the first arms stretched toward him
Eagerness of young girl reaching for doll,
archetype of mother counting tiny toes.

And always, after Mary, the yearning.
The whole human smorgasbord of wants:
for a mate. For a child. For health, a job.
God's answer to the long desire: Jesus.
Never slick nor easy as we might want,
no clean signature on the dotted line.

God's response to us like God's to Mary:
I give you my son. I give you all that is
best of me. I give you promise, hope,
potential. All that is God shrunk smaller
than a ten-pound sack of potatoes:
Limp. Wobbly. Soft. Sleepy. Warm.

God's syllogism: if I could trust Mary,
I can trust you with the finest. Harbor
him in your supple arms.

Question for Discussion or Reflection

◆ At Christmas we often get so caught up in our own celebration, we sometimes overlook the meaning of the feast. If
you're not reading this during the Christmas season, what
is the effect of reflecting on the nativity at another time
of year?

Chapter Six

The Later Triptych:
Cana, Calvary, Easter

Cana

THE STORY OF Jesus' first miracle tells us a great deal about Mary. In the context of a loving relationship, a refusal to help seems hurtful and hard to understand. How, then, did Mary feel when, seeing the wedding wine run out, she asked Jesus to help at Cana, and he replied, "My hour has not yet come"?

She responded with an apparent contradiction: despite Jesus' seeming to deny her request, she still told the waiters, "Do whatever he tells you." Mary sensed the "yes" beneath what sounded distinctly like "no." She trusted implicitly that Jesus knows what he's doing, as we all must.

In John's Gospel, Mary is mentioned only twice, at Cana and at Calvary. She is never identified by name, called only the mother of Jesus, whom he addressed formally as "woman." We might translate that as "my lady." At Cana, his hour hadn't yet come; at Calvary, the hour has arrived. Both instances occurred at wedding feasts. In the first (chapter 2), water turns to wine. In the second (chapter 19), blood and water pour from Jesus' side, wedding him to humanity as its savior.

Another echo of Cana comes in John 21:20–23. At the wedding feast, Jesus dismissed Mary's observation somewhat brusquely, saying: "What is it to you?" Those words recur after the resurrection, when Peter asked about the beloved disciple. Jesus answered in the same vein: "What is it to you?" Some interpret this to mean, "Dismiss anxiety. Focus on your own life with God. Trust God to do whatever will bring you closer together. But don't compare yourself with anyone else!"

Modeling Mary, we too are called to intervene when we see human need. She showed us that following Jesus isn't a matter of passivity, but of taking the initiative. God always wants our participation when God acts in human events. As one Scripture scholar writes: "God waits on our invitation to act.... Certainly Jesus found his mother's behind-the-scenes preparation for the miracle at Cana an offer he could not refuse, however put out he may have felt about the hour not being quite right."[34]

Calvary

It has been mentioned before that the focus of this book is not so much on what sets Mary apart or makes her special, but on what makes her like us. We have studied how she pondered in her heart the unfolding experiences that surprised her, trying to find meaning in them. Her stance is no different when she enters the hardest part of her life, the suffering and death of her son. Her intimacy with him there must have deepened what Alice Camille calls "the boundless tenderness and empathy with which she was destined to console the afflicted of human history."[35]

To see the passion of Jesus through his mother's eyes is to experience it in a new way. For Mary, the mother's most urgent cry, "Don't hurt my child!" is violated. It is impossible for her to look on passively, independent of his suffering. As every mom knows, each scraped knee or bumped head a child experiences touches her to the quick. If sympathy pains are possible, mothers feel them for their offspring. In his poem "Good Friday: Riding Westward," written in 1613, John Donne describes her as:

> ... God's partner here, and furnished thus,
> Halfe of that Sacrifice, which ransomed us....

In a small glimpse of what Mary endured, I once worried about a dear friend who was reenacting the way of the cross with a peace and justice group on Good Friday. They would walk to various stations where Christ's passion continues: the immigration office, the courthouse, the soup kitchen, the food stamp office, the homeless shelter, the health clinic. At each they would stop and pray, making the connection between daily routines for poor people and the way Christ continues to suffer today.

This admirable procession wended through four miles of the downtown area with 120 committed people. But at a distance, I worried about my friend. He'd had heart surgery two months before: Would the walk be too exhausting? Could he carry a six-foot cross that far? The March winds were chilly and bitter that day: Had he worn a warm coat? Such anxieties are probably silly; as it turned out, a homeless person helped him carry the cross. But what I imagined from afar gives a tiny indication of what Mary's thoughts must have been, watching closely as Jesus walked the actual way of the cross.

Presentations of the Passion through dance show Mary's figure interwoven with Jesus', bearing every insult, feeling every blow. It may be a cliché, but it is the heartfelt wish of the parent who sees the child suffer: Let me take the pain instead. Let me suffer in his or her place. The agony for Mary must have been knowing she could do nothing to stop the torture or to take Jesus' place. Her role was simply to stand beside him while he endured the terrible ordeal that saved us.

> *Mary weeps again over the swollen, starved corpse of a child in Darfur. Patiently, she attends a son's trial in Dallas, and cringes as he receives the death penalty. Instinctively she knows from the doorbell in the middle of the night and the presence of soldiers on the porch that her child has been killed at war.*

What must it have meant to him to have her there? On the simplest plane, we know that when we must endure a dreaded dental procedure or undergo surgery, the edge is less sharp when someone we love is with us. Seeing Mary at the foot of the cross must have consoled Jesus, but at the same time broken his heart. He would not want her to suffer, yet he would want her there, she who had shared intimately his first thirty years of life and, at a little distance, the last three.

The figure of the *mater dolorosa,* or sorrowful mother, symbolizes women's inherent opposition to violence. "The *mater dolorosa* stands for the refusal to subordinate pain to tales of victory and defeat."[36] In other words, the Roman centurion may have gone home and boasted of an efficient crucifixion outside of Jerusalem. His wife, hearing the tale, unless she was completely brainwashed by the "glorious stories of valor," might have turned aside in disgust.

Women reject violence because they know the cost of human flesh, having borne it at great cost within their own bodies. Their alienation from "men's wars" was expressed in the 1930s by Virginia Woolf, who demanded of men: don't fight to protect me or "our country." "As a woman...my country is the whole world." We are skeptical of branding someone "the enemy" who loves and protects their children as we do, who hates the idea of killing as much as we do, who might happily cooperate in the building of a global society if it weren't for the crazy rhetoric used to justify war. "Maternal attentive love, restrained and clear-sighted, is ill adapted to intrusive, let alone murderous, judgments of others' lives."[37]

While mothers can be just as racist and hateful as anyone else, they "*struggle* toward nonviolence, *struggle* not to hurt what is strange, not to let other children be abused out of fear or loyalty to one's own."[38] We see Mary's role reprised again and again as the Mothers of the Disappeared protest in Latin American countries, carrying their sad pictures of children lost to repressive regimes. These women wear identical masks to mark their commonality. In Chile, one mother said of the group, "If we find one disappeared one I will rejoice as much as if they had found mine."[39]

Mary weeps again over the swollen, starved corpse of a child in Darfur. Patiently, she attends a son's trial in Dallas, and cringes as he receives the death penalty. Instinctively she knows from the doorbell in the middle of the night and the presence of soldiers on the porch that her child has been killed at war. Mourning, she wonders what kind of half-life she will lead without this son or daughter on whom the sun rose and set.

A Spanish painting, *Costado,* depicts Jesus leaning forward from the cross, toward a figure who could only be Mary. Both are portrayed in a warm yellow glow. The artwork inspired this poem:

Images from the Cross:
Jesus to His Mother

They have me pinned, but I shall bend.
Nails could no more block this flow
than sticks could stop a river. Seeing
her below, I lean forward as John once
leaned on my breast, as Spirit once
overshadowed her. She looks young and
small as she did then — such costly love.

The most savage torture, surpassing
any cruelty the Romans could devise:
not being wrenched open myself
but against my will, involving her,
hideous contagion, as if I had invited
murderous thugs into our home
or poured acidic poison on her skin.

On this wood, the jagged graffiti of blood.
Message carved into my skin, I the
envelope ripped apart like onion skin.
My moan of agony the music of creation.

Like crooning mother over cradle, I
gasp lullaby in melodies she once sang,
wear her posture, her terrible tenderness.

She who taught me how to birth
finishes the labor now, bold midwife.
She would never abort the end nor let
me shudder with contractions alone.
As I dim, she lifts the torch: dark radiance.
As I despair, she trusts enough for two,
fierce lioness. Abandoned? No — accompanied.

Easter

Many people, like St. Ignatius of Loyola, believed that Jesus'
first appearance after the resurrection was to Mary. Indeed,
Acts 1:3 mentions Jesus appearing to many other people.
Knowing his closeness to Mary, it's easy to imagine the joy of
his reunion with her.

Picture, for instance, the kindergartener who has won a
blue ribbon for his art project. He can't wait to get home
and share it with his mother. So too, the high school student
receiving high SAT scores or winning a tennis tournament.
He or she may saunter into the house with optimum cool, but
beneath the surface runs an urgency: tell mom the good news.
Phone lines vibrate with the words, "You're a grandmother
now!" And then the cycle begins again: "Grandma, I got a
puppy!"

These human examples give a glimpse of how Jesus must
have rushed to Mary after his resurrection. She had endured
so much with him, it is fitting that she should share his victory

over death. Although this appearance may not be recorded in Scripture, it carries the weight of inner truth and popular belief. Rainer Maria Rilke writes in "Mary at Peace with the Risen Lord": "Oh to her first."

Such joy cannot be contained in words, but spills into song. The "Regina Coeli," a Marian anthem for Eastertide, sings:

> Joy fill your heart, O Queen most high, Alleluia!
> Your son who in the tomb did lie, alleluia!
> Has risen as he did prophesy, alleluia!
> Pray for us, Mother, when we die, alleluia!

An antiphon from the glorious mysteries repeats that refrain: "Rejoice and be glad, O Virgin Mary, alleluia, / For the Lord has truly risen, alleluia."

Ann Johnson writes a "Magnificat of Resurrection," based on John 20:19–21. In it Mary's soul again delights and rejoices, because God has removed the stone rolled over our hearts. The Almighty has called us forth from death, enfeebled the mighty rulers, and empowered the simple people who trust. The triumph of the apparently weak over the baffled soldiers of the mighty Roman Empire exemplifies what Mary had predicted: "You throw down the mighty from their thrones and exalt the lowly."

The anguished are "stilled and made whole again by this good news." Mary echoes her original song, showing how God has again come to the help of Israel, and concludes, "You are the Forever Living One, the Shatterer of Death." How appropriate that Mary would sing the same canticle at the beginning of Jesus' earthly life and the beginning of eternal life. Both events are totally unexpected, yet prompt an outpouring of praise. As the brackets surrounding all lives, birth and death should be heralded with joy. Once again, Mary leads the way.

Questions for Discussion or Reflection

+ Imagine that you could speak to Mary at one of these three junctures in her life: Cana, Calvary, or Easter. Which one would you choose?

+ What would you say?

Chapter Seven

Mary as Mother—
and Her Long Maternal Line

RECENT RESEARCH and writing that seek to understand
the "mother-line" of spiritual awareness and the nature
of mothering contribute new insights to our understanding of
Mary. Let's begin by placing her within that line of women
that stretches back to Sarah and Hannah and forward into
our own times.

The Foremothers

"There are families in South India that trace their ancestry
back through the maternal line, and a friend who grew up
in one of these clans used to swear that right along with the
DNA, spiritual awareness flows down the mother-line ... 'like
a river.' "[40] Women today stand squarely in Mary's lineage. It
includes some formidable women who came before us and
cheer us on: Esther, Deborah, Mary Magdalene, Lydia, Cath-
erine of Siena, Hildegard of Bingen, Teresa of Avila, Elizabeth
Ann Seton, Katharine Drexel, Dorothy Day, Thea Bowman.
They are a powerful "cloud of witnesses" that understand the
human struggle and support us through it. Each represents,
within her own time and culture, a flowering of compassion,

generosity, and creativity that mark her as a descendant of Mary. "Like mother, like daughter."

Now we continue this flow of abundant grace and virtue. The support of other women has contributed significantly to the contemporary flowering of women's art, poetry, music, and drama, and enhanced roles in science, politics, medicine, and business. While advances in those fields garner most of the attention, quieter support systems also thrive: a mother telling her daughter she needn't endure an abusive husband; a sister who fills in for the mother of an autistic child, giving the caregiver a much-needed break; women whose gifts take the form of listening intently, parenting well, being a faithful friend or spouse. The rallying cry of black women in South Africa describes their community: "You have struck the women; you have struck the rock."

Those familiar with the Communion of Saints will recognize this dynamic. Neither time nor space can block its hidden channel of inspiration, encouragement, and protection. Mentors may live in a different era or distant place, but women still connect with older and younger people whom they may or may not be related to, supporting their dreams and undertakings as professors, scientists, journalists, artists, musicians, mothers, teachers, healers, diplomats, and designers.

Mary's Mantle

Artists represent Mary wearing a huge mantle that shelters many people beneath its folds. As Kathleen Norris writes, "There's a lot of *room* in Mary."[41] Whether we think of her in Japanese kimono or the *tilma* of Guadalupe, the image is spacious. "It embodies the breadth of compassion that comes with having swept all counterfeit identities out of the way so that, in the words of the Taoist seer, 'within herself there is room for everything' ... embodiment of female strength, resilience, compassion, and resistance."[42] Having nurtured one phenomenal child, Mary continues to nurture all her children.

While many in our church and society seem bent on excluding, Mary encourages us to *include*. Jesus' propensity for welcoming the least desirable must have come from his mother. Her mantle shelters a very large family. Marian legend typically shows her protecting those who have been kicked out by church or society. She who welcomed shepherds and magi to an intimate family event wouldn't be likely to hoist a "Keep Out" sign. The unexpected events of her life exploded safe presumptions and narrow confines. Karl Rahner could have been describing Mary when he writes that if God doesn't "call us out of the little house of our homely, close-hugged truths ... we have misunderstood the words of Christianity." After Mary's cozy walls were blown apart by the Spirit's winds, she couldn't pretend that anyone else had control, or even the ability to protect her own child.

She might well have led the little band of women who approached her son's tomb wondering, "Who will roll away the stone?" They don't let the unanswered question deter them. For thirty-three years, Mary had perfected the art of walking with the questions and welcoming Jesus' unexpected guests into the spacious home of her soul. She would have come to the tomb with the same hope she expressed in the Magnificat. There she focused not on the dastardly things humans have done, but on the terrific things God has done. With her identity firmly anchored in God's fidelity, she doesn't count on flimsy hopes like humans being "nice." A number of events in her life ruled out that airy possibility, starting with the slaughter of the innocents and ending with the crucifixion. She lives within the roomy space of absolute trust and calls us to do the same.

The Art of Mothering

Contemporary scholars writing about the nature of mothering may not mention Mary explicitly. But she could stand as the finest example of the maternal art they have researched. The marvelous configurations of hormones, cells, and skills that comprise a mother's bond with her baby must have been designed by God to someday guard and nurture God's son, Jesus.

In *Maternal Thinking,* Sara Ruddick defines the concept of attentive love, which is unique to mothers. This quality is dedicated to understanding someone else, who is definitely not the self, but who sometimes feels like an extension of the self. A mother may experience the child's fall, flu, or surgery as if the pain were her own.

Yet at the same time, she must recognize the otherness, the uniqueness of her offspring. Unconditional love can't get in the way of socializing that young person to be acceptable in his or her culture. (Consider, for instance, Mary's rebuke to Jesus when he gets lost in the temple. She must teach him that it's simply not acceptable to vanish without a word, causing your heartsick parents untold worry for three days.) This particular kind of love "allows others to be fully and freely themselves, even when that means allowing them to walk right on out the door!"[43] (Or in Mary's case, to watch him walk right up the hill of Calvary. . . .)

Attentive love knows another *without* finding the self in her. Observing her child emerge as an independent person, she delights in that person's otherness: "to see her quirky, delighted, determined independent being and let it be."[44] This emergent self is *not* the fantasy of what mom would like the child to be, but what the child really is. She tries to know her child without finding her traits in his. When the mother allows the child that independence, it leads to appropriate trust between them. "Trusting herself and her child, she can express and hear the pain of betrayal."[45]

> *With her identity firmly anchored in God's fidelity, she doesn't count on flimsy hopes like humans being "nice."*

Jesus probably didn't become what Mary had in mind. Could she ever have dreamed that her kind and sensitive boy would die naked between two thieves, crucified in excruciating pain as a criminal? While her jolting experience is the worst extreme, no child completely fulfills a parent's fantasy. And if he or she did, it's questionable whether that person would remain true to self.

Furthermore, "attentive love...rewards a faith that love will not be destroyed by knowledge, that to the loving eye the lovable will be revealed."[46] (This way of looking at people is not only emotionally and spiritually sustaining, but also concretely informative.) It accords with the essence of mysticism: to see the other person as sacred. Ultimately, that kind of view is the only way war will end. Everyone Jesus met was beloved; he might have learned this attitude from his mother.

Contemporary thinkers identify the mother's role as fostering a child's complex developing spirit, mind, heart, and body. Much as the mother wants to understand her child, she must also allow this person she is so close to a mystery, a privacy. "A child's reality is revealed only to the patient eye of love," says Iris Murdoch. "And the child grew in wisdom, age, and grace" says Luke (2:40), whom some scholars think might have consulted Mary as his source for describing Jesus' early hidden years.

What kind of home must Jesus have come from, what kind of mothering must Mary have given him, that he became so extraordinary, even on a human plane? If we set aside for a moment his divinity and consider him strictly as human, Jesus was still remarkable. He represents the fullness of humanity to which the rest of us aspire. Watching him grow and develop, Mary, like every mother, was torn between welcoming and regretting change. She knew that as she let the child into her heart, she also prepared to let him go. Each day, Jesus grew away from her. This push-pull dynamic is explained by the lens of attentive love.

Maternal love is a unique blend of holding close for protection and at the same time being willing to relinquish control. "Of the various kinds of wisdom that . . . flow down through those mother-lines, it may be the most critical."[47] At Christmas and the crucifixion, important bookends of Mary's life, we see heightened representations of both extremes. At key times, she guards the infant from death and lets the adult fulfill his reason for being, no matter how dreadfully wrong his brutal death must seem. Mary's relinquishment on Calvary

dramatizes "a profound letting go that is directly propor-
tionate to an immense welling up of grace and light and
sustenance."[48]

When from the cross Jesus gives Mary into the care of the
beloved disciple and him into her safekeeping, it represents
his giving her to all of us. Thus, her relinquishment of *one*
child leads to her mothering of *all* children. We've observed it
casually at a playground or a school crossing: mothers instinctively protect the lives of other children besides their own.
So Mary becomes mother of *all* humanity. We know that she
must have played a key role in the early Christian community,
keeping them faithful to what Jesus wanted. Her input would
have been absolutely crucial to keep them on target. Now we
know that this role has implications for all older women.

The Grandmother Role

Anthropologists who study the role of older women in primitive societies have developed the "grandmother hypothesis,"
which is widely debated, but also accepted enough to justify
its inclusion here. For hunter-gatherers, it's the mother's job
to feed the children. "The harder she forages, the more weight
her children gain."[49] But that correspondence changes when
the mother has a newborn to feed. Lactation demands that
the mother increase her calorie intake, so she must eat most
of what she gathers. Therefore, the care of the other children
shifts to another older female. Usually it's her mother, but
often it can be an older aunt, cousin, or great-aunt.

These older women don't restrict their care to grandchildren. They help *any* child who needs it, enhancing the
health of the whole group. Some scientists believe that women,

unlike other primates, have menopause because they aid human survival more in their role as helpers to new mothers than they would if they continued to have children themselves. By sharing the burden of feeding children, humans freed themselves to explore the world and develop an intelligence and creativity far surpassing any other primates. "What distinguishes women from other primates, then, isn't menopause but the long, robust life that women can lead after menopause."[50]

So humans are programmed to rely on an older woman. Iris, who is now a grandmother, remembers vividly how as a Protestant child in Kansas, she saw nuns for the first time. Her father was seriously ill in the rural area's only hospital. The little girl was frightened by the long dresses and elaborate headgear she'd never seen on women. Day after day, she sat in the waiting room because the rules prohibited a five-year-old from going upstairs to visit her father.

Then one day, as Iris agonized over the cruel separation, Sister Liguori Roth appeared in front of her. "What are you doing here?" she asked. When Iris explained, sister scooped her up and said, "I run this place. Come with me." She escorted her past all the gatekeepers, into her father's room. Seventy years later, Iris still cherishes the memory of that sister, a competent — and compassionate — hospital administrator.

Most women going to therapists seek one who is female and older. "A woman's mother-lust, her need for the older female and for other women generally, is also ancient, and also worth heeding."[51] While fathers, among most primates, have little to do with child-rearing (our society seems to be changing that pattern) females have always formed a solid core that assures that no one grows hungry. One writer describes graphically how this theory affects her relationship with her daughter:

> I hope that I'm right in my interpretation of the organic grandmother, that mother hunger is a primal trait of womanness, and that my daughter's need for me may prove larger, more enduring and more passionate than the child's need for meals, clothes, shelter and applause.... May she spit fire and leave me gladly, but sense in her very hemoglobin that she can find me and rest with me and breathe, safely breathe, if only for the fleeting intermission between cycles of anger and disappointment.[52]

Rev. Susan Harriss enlarges this idea, from a Christian mother's standpoint, by showing the close connection between "terrified" and "terrific." The women at Jesus' tomb were terrified. So are most new parents, confronting overwhelming challenges and responsibilities. Gradually, setting aside their own interests for their child's, they become pretty terrific.

But they would also be terrified if their life's work were judged solely on their parenting. If our children were everything, how would we ever let them go? Furthermore, many women live thirty years beyond their children's leaving home. "What kind of God would assign to a human being a role that only takes part of her life and leaves the rest of her time on earth as a kind of emptiness?"[53]

The resolution Harriss reaches is this: we learn how to touch, tend, care, love, through our children. But that is only practicing the scales. We play the concerto when we transfer our love to all humanity. "Now the music begins. . . . Now we rise to the task for which our parenting prepared us. . . . Although we lost ourselves in our mothering, God remembered us, and brought us forward, and made us new."[54] As older women make this transition, which is also as Harriss implies, a kind of resurrection, Mary is their first, best guide.

Storytelling

Mothers have a special way of passing on information. They tell stories, a respectful strategy that encourages another person to trust his or her own observation and intuition. "Here's what happened to me and wasn't I surprised" is much less authoritarian than "here's what you have to do."

In their conversations "mothers refine their capacity for concrete ways of knowing, practicing together attentive noticing and disciplined reflectiveness about what they notice."[55] That strikes a familiar chord from Luke's Gospel: "And Mary treasured all these things, pondering them in her heart" (2:19). A mother's stories, pieced together from her family's activities, give her children the confidence that they have a life which is both their own and connected with others. These stories are filled with both change and reassuring continuities.

Children are shaped by the stories they're first told. So Jesus must have heard from Mary about his people: Abraham and Sarah, Moses and Miriam. From his mother, he came to know his heritage and learned to take his place among his people, as the savior they had long anticipated.

A mother remembers the whole line of her child's life, even parts the child doesn't remember. Who *else* could recount so accurately, in loving detail, "The Day You Were Born" or

"How You Took Your First Tumble Down the Porch Steps"? With her son Jesus, Mary placed those particulars into the context of the larger Story, God's repeated, saving interventions with the Hebrew people. She knew her son would play a remarkable role in that Story, even though she probably didn't understand it fully. So all mothers encourage their extraordinary children — and isn't every child extraordinary?

That storytelling tradition continues. No one has played a greater role in passing along the essence of Christianity than those who remember and retell the stories of Jesus. And who was more likely than the women to "gather the people, tell the stories, and break the bread"?

As Luke 24:1–13 implies, the women's memories preserve the community of faith. The pivotal word of the angel at the tomb is "Remember. . . . " The future hinges on the women remembering how Jesus had predicted his death and resurrection. Japanese-American poet Janice Mirikitani believes the women at the tomb bring hope to all people told to keep quiet, threatened not to reveal family secrets, ordered not to disrupt complacent silence. She describes the female witness to the resurrection, like Mary, who: "with the throat full of grace / tells us truth. . . . Her words breaking like light."[56]

Contemporary Examples — the Mother-Line Continues

Scientists who study the human brain know that connections which we use often are strengthened; others weaken as we use them less. The experience of mothering creates dramatic change in the brain, because the stakes are high. Nature has programmed the new mother to ensure the survival of the species. In other words, it helps to have someone smart looking out for the smallest, most vulnerable humans.

A mother's experiences after giving birth are emotionally powerful and sensory-rich. Her brain then is rapidly forming new neurons and connections, a phenomenon scientists call *plasticity.* "There are certainly times in life when there are windows in brain development, when the brain is more plastic than at other times. Motherhood is one of those times," says David Lyons at Stanford University. Furthermore, she doesn't forget this learning. Picture a grandmother with a new baby: she knows instinctively how to cuddle and rock the infant.

Scientists who have taken blood samples of mothers stroking or breastfeeding their infants have found an increase of the chemical oxytocin in the bloodstream.[57] This chemical creates a feeling of calm, exhilaration, and joy. And don't most people want to repeat a pleasurable sensation?

Nature has other ways of strengthening the mother's attachment to the child. A gorilla baby arrives with almost no fat; a human baby is fat because it makes him or her look rounded, fleshy, adorable. Natalie Angier writes, "The visual seductions of a baby, its cuteness quotient, may magnify its power to win the warmth, the nose, the touch, the low-fat holy water of its mother."[58]

Human senses and systems are designed to remind a mother of attachments imprinted on her mind and body. Even the thought of her infant can stimulate a nursing mother to produce milk. Another stimulus for attachment is that stray cells from the fetus stay within the mother's body decades after she has given birth. That gives new meaning to the song, "There's Always Something There to Remind Me"!

Immigrant mothers who make dangerous ocean or desert crossings are often motivated by the desire to give their children a better future. They are among the most dramatic examples of mothers who have always done brave and generous things for their offspring. Anger and assertiveness can be effective tools for protecting the young. (Surely Mary took this stand when she fled to Egypt to protect her child from Herod.) "Mom Radar," keenly aware of any threat to the young, springs from a strong attachment developed even before the baby's birth.

This maternal stance continues, as mothers take on causes, organizing against drunk driving, advertising that exploits kids, violence, drugs, and war. In 1988, Sister Helen Prejean connected a support group for murder victims' families with an anti-death penalty group, and named the new entity Survive. She marveled at the resilience of black mothers who had lost their children to murder. For them, the motto "God makes a way out of no way" was not simply a pious sentiment, but a way of life. While Mary's presence among those who guard and mourn the young may not be explicit, it's not hard to imagine Mary's banner waving over her daughters united to make the world better for their children.

Furthermore, some sectors of the workplace have recognized that the skills developed by mothers transfer well to jobs: for instance, juggling multiple tasks and responsibilities, reading nonverbal signals (like a baby's urgency for milk or a dry diaper), recognizing a larger world than the career, developing empathy, creativity, patience, and the ability to delegate.

For many animals, and especially for humans, separation from offspring causes distress, with perceptibly higher levels of stress hormones circulating in their bloodstreams. Tests on rats show them overcoming huge obstacles simply to be reunited with their young. In the human arena, we know how Mary suffered when separated from Jesus. When mother and child are together, great things spring from their happiness. For example, St. Clare's mother joined her in the San Damiano convent. Julian of Norwich mentions during her Revelations that her mother is there beside her.

Jane Goodall discovered a super-mom among the chimpanzees of Africa and named her Flo. Observing her for several decades, Goodall realized how the chimp's daughter Fifi absorbed the same qualities and exercised them as a mother herself. She calls it a "spectacular mother-line — confident, resilient, and good-natured."[59]

Intriguingly, Goodall may have known what to look for because she herself was the product of such a nurturing, female environment. She often says, "I come from a long line of strong, compassionate women." Indeed, it was her mother, Vanne, who accompanied Jane to Africa, because a young woman traveling by herself would have been suspect.

While her example may be more dramatic than most, Vanne was simply providing what mothers should always offer daughters: solid, loving, reliable backup. How many mothers have babysat the grandchildren so their daughters could continue their educations? In the best scenarios, mother steps in whenever she can to support her daughter's trajectory.

In a healthy mother-daughter relationship, each one relaxes in the company of the other, dropping the defenses and social mechanisms employed in other relationships. No need to create a false front with one who changed our diapers, or with one who will care for us in old age.

Giving an annual mother-daughter retreat around Mother's Day with my daughter has given me a place from which to observe many mother-daughter relationships. In many ways, some quite funny, these pairs exhibit what the scholars like to call a preference for concrete rather than abstract thinking. One daughter, for instance, described her mom's loyalty: "My first job was selling subscriptions to a magazine that was mostly fluff. That didn't bother mom. She persuaded twelve of her friends to subscribe!"

Another daughter spoke of an ectopic pregnancy that caused her so much pain she wouldn't get out of bed. As her condition worsened, her husband tried harder to get her to a doctor, but she refused to budge. Desperate, he phoned her mother. When mom arrived on the scene and saw what was happening, she didn't waste any time. "Get up and get dressed," she told her daughter. "We're going to the hospital." And, amazing even her herself, daughter complied. Long after the crisis, the daughter laughed: "Mom was the only one in the world who could have done that!"

Throughout Ann Patchett's novel *Run* recurs the theme of a Mary statue, with auburn hair and Irish features like the women of the family who have passed down this heirloom for centuries. Two African American boys treasure the statue because it reminds them of their adoptive mother who died when they were small. They long to inherit it, but the statue is eventually given to a young African American girl, whom they think a sister. Unknown to them, she is really unrelated, due to a long series of complications. The simple explanation for the bequest? "You're the daughter."

The same might be said to all women who honor Mary. You're the daughter. You look like her. So? Live like her.

"Just as any star needs its aura to shine, so Mary needs to be placed within the multitude of women throughout history to manifest her true greatness."[60] In other words: as a woman's identity is enriched by those she has birthed and/or nurtured, so Mary is completed by her many daughters and sons. As their numbers swell beneath her infinitely expansive mantle, so she grows in beauty and strength. Mary and her son Jesus give us the templates: this is what it means to be a fully developed woman or man. It's our job to mirror and complete them. Mary's best qualities shine forth in us; we find our truest, best selves in her.

Between human mothers and daughters tensions, disagreements, misunderstandings can arise. Even with these limitations, the relationship gives us clues of how we stand with respect to Mary. If a daughter inherits her mother's ability with pottery, numbers, words, music, or gardens, it's easy to trace the source to a childhood steeped in such treasures, where such talents were valued. Children growing up with artists, for instance, find it natural to dabble with paint.

The same is true for less tangible qualities: serenity, humor, graciousness, strength under pressure, different kinds of intelligence. "We know where you got that!" we smile, recognizing in the next generation a trait exhibited in a previous one. We all stand within a flowing current; every now and then, we recognize our inheritance.

Questions for Discussion or Reflection

♦ Is the "mother-line" a new concept for you?

♦ Do you feel that you stand within it?

• How have you felt its influences?

• Name and reflect on a woman who has nurtured you or protected you. She need not be biologically related. What did she give you?

• Does she help you to understand Mary in some way? Why or why not?

• While this chapter discusses women's achievements in many realms, it's important to remember the quiet accomplishments. As Etty Hillesum writes: "It is possible to create, even without ever writing a word or painting a picture, by simply 'molding' one's inner life. And that too is a deed."[61] To which arena have you contributed most of your energies at different times of your life?

——————————————————

Chapter Eight

Praying with Mary

WOMEN HAVE GROWN so tired of being defined by men, told what they think, like, and want to buy, that even well-meaning attempts have become laughable. "I'll sketch out my own identity, thank you very much. No matter how confused or inflated it might be, it feels familiar and it fits," we say. So having our role as women and our relationship with God modeled by another woman is cause for gratitude. That identification may account for women's traditional devotion to Mary, especially in societies more patriarchal than ours.

Mary reveals the feminine face of the divine. When God's motherly side is diminished or ignored, the whole church suffers, orphaned. So too, when women are marginalized, humankind is impoverished. We limp on one leg without the generous female gifts that God intended for all humanity. Both failures — to adequately appreciate the fullness of God and that of human beings — are healed in Mary. As Leonardo Boff writes, "The divine story of God's sympathy for human beings is incomplete without the peerless figure of Mary."[62]

Without falling into gender stereotypes, most people would agree that men and women do many things differently. Ask most guys about shopping or fashions; their eyes glaze over like those of a woman hearing a detailed description of a football play. It's logical, then, that men and women differ when it comes to prayer styles.

Praying with Mary takes on a tone unlike prayer formed by men and directed to a deity imaged as male, even prayer to Jesus. The Angelus is short, flexible, biblically based, and punctuates the day with prayer three times. At 6:00 a.m., noon, and 6:00 p.m. people stop what they're doing and turn their thoughts to God. In more traditional societies, *everyone* paused at the ringing of the Angelus bell. (Millet's famous painting shows farmers in the field setting aside carts and pitchforks to pray.) The name comes from the Latin word for angel, in the first line of the prayer: "The angel of the Lord declared unto Mary.... "

Contemporary applications have been creative. While hectic schedules may prevent the traffic-stopping that once occurred, people still step away from their desks or set their cell phone alarms to replace the church bell. Mary, who knew the stresses of daily household routines, would appreciate such efforts to regularly transform the ordinary.

The rosary, a prayer which repeats the Hail Mary on a series of beads, is also popular among many people. They meditate on the mysterious events of Jesus' life, often preceded with a scriptural verse. One college student remembers her mother's clever way of enforcing curfew. As she'd tiptoe into the house, trying not to awaken her parents, she'd discover mom, kneeling before a Mary statue in the hall, saying a rosary for her daughter's safety.

Sister Helen Prejean remembers returning from the first execution she witnessed in Angola prison: her "Catholic mama" met her at the door "with her rosary still in her hands." Prejean herself, at the heart of controversy over the death penalty, sees the rosary's symbolism: "you touch and hold each small, smooth bead, and then you let it go.... This is the great secret.... Nothing is solid. Everything moves. Except love — hold on to love. Do what love requires."[63]

The Hail Mary, which is central to both the Angelus and the rosary, has remained in the collective unconscious of Christians for centuries. The prayer is like a mantra we whisper in times of stress or a song that floats unconsciously into mind when we face difficulty.

For a long time, I quietly hummed Amy Grant's song "Breath of Heaven" whenever I needed an extra dose of spiritual strength. Sung in the imagined words of Mary, it expresses her confusion and asks for God's holiness to fill her. "Breath of heaven, hold me together," I'd whisper, approaching a health crisis for myself or someone I loved. The refrain "Pour over me your holiness, for you are holy" would sing in my head as I listened to a speaker introduce me before I gave a day of prayer. "Make me your channel. If this goes well, it's all your gift, O God," I'd pray silently as the audience looked expectantly in my direction.

In the same way, prayers to Mary have nested in human hearts and sung through human minds for centuries. In stressful times or joyful ones, people have turned instinctively to her. Many people, drawing on childhood memory, have recited the Hail Mary. It attempts to put into words a mystery that still remains elusive. It fails, as all words must, to express everything we long to say. But it succeeds in capturing a few ideas which are intrinsic to an understanding of Mary.

Overfamiliarity is the enemy of faith; if we yawn at another recitation of a prayer we've heard or said repeatedly, we may miss deeper layers of meaning within it. As Richard Rohr says, "Overexplanation separates us from astonishment." We need a middle ground where we can still be surprised by the untapped depths of the familiar. So with the guidance of theologian Leonardo Boff, let's reflect on each phrase of an ancient prayer, contemporary enough to make front page headlines when a grandmother, rosary in hand, prays to forgive her grandson's killer.

"*Ave,*" that first word of Gabriel at the Annunciation, is usually translated "Hail." Boff draws attention to the deep pool of joy that underlies the word. For centuries, humankind had awaited "the revelation that would fully embody the feminine in God.... The age-old dreams, the deepest hopes of generations, were set on this." Because the expectations finally flower in Mary, exuberance overflows. "Mary is the place where everything comes together.... The entire history of humankind converges at a decisive point in Mary."[64] One three-letter word summarizes it all.

In contemporary terms, think of the untranslatable syllable a child shouts, jumping into a swimming pool, the "all *right*" as teammates exchange high fives after a surprising victory, the understated "hi" as lovers who have been separated a long time sink into each other's arms. While none of these examples begins to touch the depth of the angel's greeting, they give us glimmers. Multiplied and combined, they hint at the fullness of Gabriel's "ave."

If we didn't already know the second word, we might suspect that on this momentous occasion, the angel would address a learned rabbi, a powerful leader, or a highly respected prophet. Instead, Mary is young, female, and oppressed — three strikes against her that weigh heavily in human terms, but apparently are insignificant to God.

The name *"Mary"* means "God's beloved." Earlier, we saw
how the name also refers to bearing the bitterness of the time.
This more positive meaning brings good news for all who
share the identity of God's beloved. We have a part in the family name and the inherited traits. In Mary, humanity, which
had been separated from God in Eden, reunites with God:
for us, the ultimate fulfillment. Because of her, nothing can
"separate us from the love of Christ" (Rom. 8:35).

Leonardo Boff says our translation *"full of grace"* misses
a fundamental dynamic: the Holy Spirit's initiative, making
Mary the Spirit's sanctuary. She becomes the home for God
Jesus might have envisioned when he encouraged his followers: "Make your home in me as I make mine in you" (John
15:4). She makes it possible for God to "pitch God's tent
among us," as John's prologue (1:14) so graphically describes
the incarnation. The beautiful epitome of Israel, Mary thus
creates the transition from the old tent of Israel, protecting
the ark of the covenant, to the new tent, the body of Christ
in our midst.

Again, to set this idea in contemporary terms: We all know
the relief of turning the corner into our own street, collapsing
into our own bed, smelling the favorite scents of the kitchen,
or looking out the window on a scene we've viewed thousands
of times. At home, we relax, renew energies, speak honestly
about the crazy world we contend with outside. Home is usually the locus for our deepest loves, strongest fears, highest
hopes. A healthy home becomes the arena for intimacy, the
launching pad for service to others and engagement with the
larger world.

Knowing the spiritual implications of the physical home,
what could it mean to make our home in another person?

It means that when we're with him or her, we're confident. No place is foreign. We can explore the farthest reaches of Antarctica, cross borders where we don't know the language, the customs or the currency, because the tension of the unknown is mitigated by the warm presence at our side. Scary adventure, unexplored territory, and new experience lose their dread when we can laugh together. The raw edge that usually induces insecurity is blunted by one we dearly love. Projects we would never tackle alone become doable within the secure shelter of the other.

Finding sanctuary became common coinage within the context of the immigration movement, when courageous churches and families provided safe harbors for people fleeing war, political oppression, or economic desperation. Those who have not had to leave their homes can only imagine the perilous desert or ocean crossing, the life-threatening hazards, the heart-in-throat terror of that exodus. For those who survive, it must mean the world to find water and food, safety and rest, the protection and companionship of people who aren't suspiciously bent on arrest.

Given these steps in what we know, it's still a leap of the imagination to think of Mary as sanctuary not only for the Spirit but for *us*. Within the tenderness of her care, our anxieties cease, our raving compulsions fall still, we can be at peace. When we're freed from self-defense mode, happy in the companionship of this peerless friend, we can relax and become strong, confident, the people we were created to be, like Mary.

"The Lord is with thee." I'll always remember a wonderful talk given on the feast of Mary's Assumption. The speaker's research had included asking her teen-aged daughter the

meaning of the feast. "Mary's assumption," replied the girl, "is that God would always be with her."

The only reliable door into the future, the only guarantee in human relationships, is trust. Without it, we cannot function as a society or within a family. Even those who have known an avalanche of God's blessings find themselves filled with vague, uncertain fears. Many people who attend church regularly and consider themselves Christian still face mysterious anxieties they can't explain, which usually surface at 3:00 a.m. Stories throughout Scripture relate how different biblical figures — Abraham and Sarah, Jacob, Leah and Rachel, Moses and Miriam, David, Ruth struggled to trust God and other human beings.

We continue to meet these sparks, God's presence among us, in the most ordinary, humble people and places. When we do encounter the holy we say a blessing: not to make the object holy, but to recognize the holiness already there.

Mary must have worked hard to achieve trust and was certainly placed in plenty of situations that challenged it. Just for starters: Conceive a baby without a husband? Give birth in squalor? Flee to Egypt with a young child? Lose a twelve-year-old in the temple? Watch a son mature, trying not to entertain ominous fears about his future? Freely tell a young adult goodbye, dreading where he might be going? Hear distressing rumors about that son saying things and performing cures that no one can explain? Watch him tortured and die an excruciating death? Bury him in a borrowed tomb?

If we had experienced even one of these challenges, even slightly, we can sense how heroic was Mary's trust in God. She was human, so she entertained doubt. But as far as we know, she never went back on the initial "yes" that launched her whole story, and Jesus', and ours. Her serenity must have been drawn from a deep inner conviction that God was with her — no matter how much evidence seemed to contradict that. She is full of grace because she is the vessel for God's presence.

Some of the prophets and saints receive bursts of inspiration to complete specific missions. Then, like Amos, they return to trimming the sycamore trees. But Mary becomes the permanent dwelling place for the Spirit; from her, the divine life radiates to all. Think of a giant wheel with a glowing hub at the center. From it flows energy to the furthest rim. Mary is that essential, central core. Because she is infused with God, we look to her; she keeps us turning.

"Blessed art thou among women." The words are Elizabeth's (Luke 1:42); now they jokingly refer to any man surrounded by bright, articulate female company. The word "blessed" dates back to the mystical teachings of Judaism, described by Rachel Remen in her book *My Grandfather's Blessings.*[65] At the beginning of time, God hurled sparks of the Holy throughout creation. We continue to meet these sparks, God's presence among us, in the most ordinary, humble people and places. When we do encounter the holy we say a blessing: not to *make* the object holy, but to *recognize* the holiness already there.

Mary's holiness springs from her fulfillment as God's servant, God's mother, and the representation of God's heart. Furthermore, she is the epitome of what all human beings can become. As Meister Eckhart wrote,

> What good is it to me
> if Mary is full of grace
> if I am not also full of grace?
> What good is it to me for the Creator
>   to give birth to the Son
> if I do not also give birth to him
> in my time
> and my culture?

> We are all meant to be mothers of God.[66]

The company of women takes on new meaning during crisis. One group that lightheartedly named themselves the Rosary Babes would spring into action whenever a member or a friend had a serious crisis in the family. They *did* say the rosary — in arm chairs, while sipping coffee. Their prayer motivated their action. Together they offered what people instinctively need at a difficult time: their presence, prayer, and cooking.

While the Babes and their daughters, the Chicks, might never see it this way, their casseroles, salads, muffins, and cookies became little sacraments of the ordinary. Their desire to nurture seems deeply, mysteriously tied to their femininity. When one elderly member agonized about her husband's poor health, foreseeing his death, others reassured her: "Yes, it's bad. But we'll be there!" Those who suffer or grieve feel blessed to know such women.

"And blessed is the fruit of thy womb, Jesus." One valid criticism of some Mariology is that overemphasizing Mary distracts from Jesus. The necessary corrective is contained in this line of the prayer. Mary would probably be appalled by theories that regard her as the "back door," or suggest she offers some devious approach that avoids the Father and Son. What kind of nasty God does that thinking imply?

Instead, the Hail Mary presents the two together: Jesus and Mary, forever linked, male and female, the finest representations of God in human form. In them, we see God's face — no longer distant nor punitive, but like our own faces, with the same eyes, ears, nose, and mouth. We rejoice in these two people because of what they tell us about ourselves: we too are blessed because we too are beloved of God. As the Persian poet Rumi wrote, centuries ago: "It was to enjoy this conversation that you and I were created." Like Mary we are beloved of the Beloved, hearing from God everything we most need to know.

"Holy Mary, Mother of God." Many people cringe at the word "holy." They think of stuffy, uptight, pietistic, deadly dull people whose lives revolve around the rules. Such paragons wear tightly cinched helmets; they never deviate from prescribed, proper paths. This image of holiness places it at a distant remove from where most of us live, mired in the messy realities of grocery shopping, cholesterol, car repairs, bill-paying, traffic, and spam. The only advantage of placing holiness so far beyond most of us is that it gets us off the hook. If it's a superhuman state, we can easily give up the pursuit and wander happily back to complacent mediocrity: "Pass the cheetos and hand me the remote. Ain't it great to veg out?"

Contrast to this stereotype of holiness the intensely alive, vibrant people at the center of a magnetic field that attracts others. They are funny, relaxed, at ease in their skins. Furthermore, they make extraordinary sacrifices that few people know about: financing college for a deserving niece, even though it means fewer restaurant meals, new clothes, vacations. Their radar is attuned to others, quickly catching the immediate, unspoken need. For one person, that might mean a quick shoulder massage; for another, patient, technical help with a balky computer. They set aside their interests to take time for another person, without becoming either co-dependent or whiny about it. Because they're also savvy about satisfying their own needs, they don't turn into boring, exhausted martyrs.

Imagine the most generous, lively, compassionate, heroic, fulfilled person you know. Now magnify him or her a jillion times over, as many zeros in that number as you can dream. Imagine that person coming close to you, full of kindness and concern. Go beyond all human limits, filling that person with what is most godly in the divinity. The explosive result may give you a tiny spark of what we mean by Mary's holiness.

But qualify it always: with all her sanctity, Mary is still like us because she sometimes puzzles, questions, fears, experiences all the emotions human beings have. She is not the romantic ideal of the holy cards, but a bold girl who protests the oppression of her people, a strong woman who endures exile, an empathetic mother who suffers with her son.

Just as a human mother has a profound influence on her child, so did Mary. Like any human mother she continued to give birth to her child throughout his life. She is the first person to model fully what we are all called to do: embody

God in our frail, limited, glorious, sacred human states. Not only do we want to be like her; we were born to be like her. In her, we see the ultimate purpose and fulfillment of our lives.

"Pray for us sinners now and at the hour of our death." No matter how wealthy we are in material goods, or how confident in our spiritual peace, we still have niggling needs. We must ask this friend a favor — water the plants while I'm out of town? We must call a doctor for advice about the flu symptoms; we must ask the boss for an extension on a complicated project. We ask relatives for help on dinner; we ask kind critics to read drafts of our work. Launching a fundraiser for a fine cause, we invite committee members to enrich individual gifts with the varied talents of many. Even if we sail along in professional success, we ask routinely for evaluation, suggestions to improve our performance. These "asks" are such a normal part of humble human life that it would seem absurd if they didn't enter our relationship with Mary.

Like any mother, she is quick to provide the best nurture for the hungriest kids. Because we are "sinners," bound by human limitations, unable to see the future or even to know what's best for us, Mary intervenes. We are all going, eventually, where we would prefer not to go: like Peter, to death. How much easier that passage seems when it ends with the warm welcome of a human mother, magnified infinitely.

To place this in more understandable terms, imagine coming home for a holiday, perhaps during college. You were exhausted from final exams, feeling the first sore throat, fever, and runny nose of a cold. Then flights were delayed and blizzards snarled traffic. "Bad hair day" was an understatement; you looked like a miserable refugee wandering from one unresponsive airline official to another. Your back ached, your temperature soared, and your luggage was sent to Singapore.

Finally, *finally* you got home, collapsed into the arms of a waiting mother, smelled her cooking, and tasted all the treats she'd cooked especially for you. She'd prepared a warm, cozy bed with sheets that smelled of the clean outdoors, stocked up on your favorite novels and foods, readied everything you could possibly want. You sank into long-awaited bliss and began to heal. The welcome never chilled; the novelty never wore off. Does that scenario give a slight taste of what the entrance into heaven might be like?

Questions for Discussion or Reflection

+ Which phrase of the Hail Mary strikes you most dramatically or resonates most deeply with your inner self?

+ Why do you think this is so?

+ If you disagree with any of the interpretations above, what is *your* reading of that phrase?

+ As a personalized way of praying with Mary, complete the blanks:

Mary, I don't think I can do this: _____

because _____ .

but with your help and in the love of your son, I'll try. *Amen.*

A Later Conversation

Kathy: What began as an assignment became a relationship. Through all those months of writing about you and thinking about you, Mary, you became more real, like a sister. All I can compare it to was any venture, pleasant or un-, which we go through with a friend. The companionship makes the way less steep, erases the time, and doubles the joys.

Mary: To be honest, I didn't have much hope for you at the beginning. While I knew you'd complete the assignment because you're a professional, I wasn't sure you'd ever warm to the task — or me.

K: My entry point was our shared experience of motherhood. Just as older moms advised me through teething and adolescence, you were a wiser one who had been through the whole gamut of experience yourself. When my own son was diagnosed with cancer at about the age your son died, I turned to you numbly, instinctively. Your presence stayed with me through the surgery, one mother supporting another, and exulted with me when we got the news that the cancer was probably contained in the tumor they removed.

M: Like the toddler throwing a glorious tantrum, you raged and hissed and threw yourself around when we began this project over eighteen months ago. And now we're sharing the dining room table: meals at one end, reference books, drafts and laptop at the other. In your house, it's not unusual to have "Dinner with Mary." So you've gradually calmed, slipping into that circle of peace drawn around me.

K: Your mantle, the chaplet, the rosary: maybe they are all concrete ways to express that wide, mysterious, magnetic field that surrounds you. I guess generations of my ancestors weren't wrong about you.

M: There *is* a whispered wisdom handed down the centuries, precious as a family heirloom. The hymns, the art, the devotions just hint at the gathered treasure. They are all pointers to the person, just as the signs mark the way to the airport.

K: I think of my friends, who struggle with everything from finances to cancer to job insecurity to teenagers to elderly relatives to aging themselves. They would like to know you, to have you as a serene and stable bulwark in their lives. Maybe my readers would too. This work is a gift to them.

M: You're giving *me* the last word? You've come a long way, baby! Sure — it's a big mantle, spacious enough for everyone. Y'all come.

Notes

Chapter 1 / Mary for All Seasons

1. Herbert O'Driscoll, *Portrait of a Woman* (New York: Seabury, 1981), 47.
2. Ibid., 78.
3. John Lynch, from "A Woman Wrapped in Silence" in *Divine Inspiration: The Life of Jesus in World Poetry,* ed. Robert Atwan et al. (New York: Oxford University Press, 1998), 316–18.
4. Demetrius Dumm, *A Mystical Portrait of Jesus: New Perspectives on John's Gospel* (Collegeville, Minn.: Liturgical Press, 2001), 28.
5. Ibid., 29.
6. Elizabeth Johnson, *Truly Our Sister: A Theology of Mary in the Communion of Saints* (New York: Continuum, 2003), 303.

Chapter 2 / A Cluster of Images

7. Dorothee Soelle in Caroline Ebertshauser et al., *Mary throughout the Ages* (New York: Crossroad, 1998), 144.
8. Jim Forest, ed., *Mother Maria Skobtsova: Essential Writings* (Maryknoll, N.Y.: Orbis Books, 2003), 70.
9. Elizabeth Johnson, *She Who Is* (New York: Crossroad, 1993), 103.

Chapter 3 / Mary around the World

10. Michael O'Neill McGrath, *Blessed Art Thou* (Franklin Park, Ill.: World Library, 2004), n.p.
11. Esther De Waal, *Lost in Wonder: Rediscovering the Spiritual Art of Attentiveness* (Collegeville, Minn.: Liturgical Press, 2003), 28.
12. Ebertshauser et al., *Mary throughout the Ages,* 144.
13. Santiago Cortés-Sjöberg, "Madre Mia," *U.S. Catholic,* October 2007, 38.
14. Esther De Waal, *The Celtic Vision* (Liguori, Mo.: Liguori, 1988), xxvii.
15. Ibid., xxvi.
16. Ibid., 39.

17. Ibid., 121.

18. Ebertshauser et al., *Mary throughout the Ages,* 144.

Chapter 4 / She Who Holds the Tension

19. Jean Mambrino, *Land of Evening* (London: Enitharmon Press, 2004), 123.

20. Rosemary Ruether, *Mary — The Feminine Face of the Church* (Philadelphia: Westminster Press, 1977), 64–65.

21. Ibid., 45.

22. "Constitution on the Church," no. 67, *Vatican II in Plain English: The Constitutions,* trans. Bill Huebsch (Allen, Tex.: Thomas More, 1996), 67.

23. Quoted in "The Mystery of Mary," *Life* (December 1996): 45.

24. Madeleine L'Engle, "A Sky Full of Children" in *Watch for the Light: Readings for Advent and Christmas* (Maryknoll, N.Y.: Orbis Books, 2004), 79–81.

Chapter 5 / The Earlier Triptych

25. Denise Levertov, *The Stream and the Sapphire* (New York: New Directions, 1997), 59.

26. Ladislas Orsy, "A Time to Ponder," *America,* February 5, 2007, 16.

27. Quoted in James Keane, "The Surprise Child," *America,* December 10, 2007, 29.

28. Quoted in "The Mystery of Mary," 58.

29. Philip Yancey, "The Visited Planet" in *Watch for the Light,* 258.

30. William Willimon, "The God We Hardly Knew," in *Watch for the Light,* 149.

31. Loretta Ross-Gotta, "To Be Virgin," in *Watch for the Light,* 99.

32. Keane, "The Surprise Child," 29.

33. Evelyn Underhill, "The Light of the World," in *Watch for the Light,* 173.

Chapter 6 / The Later Triptych: Cana, Calvary, Easter

34. Alice Camille, "Immaculate Perceptions," *U.S. Catholic,* May 2006, 35.

35. Ibid.

36. Sara Ruddick, *Maternal Thinking: Toward a Politics of Peace* (New York: Ballantine Books, 1989), 140.

37. Ibid., 150.

38. Ibid., 57.

39. Ibid., 231.

Chapter 7 / Mary as Mother — and Her Long Maternal Line

40. Carol Flinders, *Enduring Lives* (New York: Tarcher/Penguin, 2006), 3.

41. Kathleen Norris, *Meditations on Mary* (New York: Viking Studio, 1999), 25.

42. Flinders, *Enduring Lives*, 255.

43. Ibid., 127.

44. Ruddick, *Maternal Thinking*, 121–22.

45. Ibid., 123.

46. Flinders, *Enduring Lives*, 131.

47. Ibid., 127.

48. Ibid., 332.

49. Natalie Angier, *Woman: An Intimate Geography* (New York: Anchor Books, 1999), 242.

50. Ibid., 246.

51. Ibid., 257.

52. Ibid., 258.

53. Susan Harriss, "More Life, More Life: On Parenting," in *The Book of Women's Sermons*, ed. Lee Hancock (New York: Riverhead, 1999), 141.

54. Ibid., 142.

55. Ruddick, *Maternal Thinking*, 98.

56. Janice Mirikitani, "Her Face," in *Journey to Joy*, ed. Andrew Walker (New York: Paulist Press, 2001), Station II.

57. Angier, *Woman*, 344.

58. Ibid., 348.

59. Flinders, *Enduring Lives*, 104.

60. Leonardo Boff, *Praying with Jesus and Mary* (Maryknoll, N.Y.: Orbis Books, 2005), 145.

61. Quoted in Flinders, *Enduring Lives*, 86.

Chapter 8 / Praying with Mary

62. Boff, *Praying with Jesus and Mary*, 144.

63. Flinders, *Enduring Lives*, 303.

64. Boff, *Praying with Jesus and Mary*, 155–56.

65. Rachel Remen, *My Grandfather's Blessings* (New York: Riverhead Books, 2000), 2–3.

66. Matthew Fox, *Meditations with Meister Eckhart* (Santa Fe: Bear & Co., 1983), 74, 81.

"Truly a spirituality for the 21st century!"
— *Dolores Leckey*

Catholic Spirituality for Adults

General Editor
Michael Leach

Forthcoming volumes include:

- *Listening to God's Word* by Alice Camille
- *Community* by Adela Gonzalez
- *Incarnation* by John Shea
- And many others.

To learn more about forthcoming titles in the series, go to *orbisbooks.com.*

For free study guides and discussion ideas on this book, go to *www.rclbenziger.com.*

Please support your local bookstore.

Thank you for reading *Mary* by Kathy Coffey. We hope you found it beneficial.